# Praise for Switched-On Sell:

"This fast moving, entertaining book shows you how to perform at your best and make more sales, faster and easier, than you ever thought possible."
**Brian Tracy,** author of *The Psychology of Selling*

"Teplitz and Alessandra show us how anyone can be a top salesperson by using their proven methods in *Switched-On Selling.* With the revolutionary Brain Gym® approach to rewiring neural pathways, old limitations evaporate, and a new path toward success becomes immediately available to catapult you to superstar status."
**Jack Canfield,** co-author of *Chicken Soup for the Soul* book series

"Before we got 'Switched-On,' we thought that the 80-20 rule—80% of sales are made by 20% of the sales force—was going to plague us forever. But immediately following the *Switched-On Selling* training, we found that all of our salespeople were achieving higher closing rates and greater profitability per sale than before. The SOS training is the only variable that changed in our sales team's training and the results are incredible! Our average salespersons' income increased by 19%. We achieved our aggressive sales goals and have been nationally recognized for attaining one of the greatest percentage of increases for two of the product lines we carry. Everyone's earnings are up and so is morale!"
**Kevin Kordek,** President & CEO, A-Active Termite & Pest Control

"No other sales book I've seen gets to the core of what drives real results more powerfully than this one. The concept of *Switched-On Selling* is brilliantly cutting-edge; Teplitz and Alessandra have combined proven scientific research with their years of experience in sales mastery to produce a book that is in a league of its own."
**Ivan Misner,** *NY Times* best-selling author and founder of BNI and Referral Institute

"Of all the Superstar authors—Tony Robbins, Jack Canfield, Mark Hansen, John Gray, Lisa Nichols, and so many others—that I have coached and assisted along their journey, Dr. Jerry Teplitz is my favorite for deep content. His immediate 'stick to the ribs,' CEO-level put-it-in-the-workplace processes can change your bottom line results in a single read. On sales and marketing, Dr. Teplitz is the leading master trainer in the world today. That's why we literally BEG Jerry to teach at our trade shows for the world's elite business leaders five times a year. Put every other read on hold until you master *Switched-On Selling;* then watch the impact this powerful training will have on your profit account next quarter."

**B.J. Dohrmann,** Founder of www.ceospace.net, bestselling author, and radio show host

"I would like to go on record as very strongly recommending both you and your *Switched-On Selling* seminar. Perhaps its greatest strength is that it doesn't require the usual follow-up, reinforcement, and retraining that most traditional methods require."

**William T. Brooks,** Master Sales Trainer, Greensboro, NC

"I highly recommend the revolutionary book *Switched-On Selling* by Jerry V. Teplitz and Tony Alessandra. As a salesperson and the author of sales books, I am most impressed with the Brain Gym® approach to rewiring the brain's neural pathways to achieve greater levels of success, confidence, and clarity than ever before. Old limitations in your sales presentation will evaporate and you will feel a renewed sense of excitement and joy. The book is an easy read and will give any salesperson new tools for being of service in the sales field."

**Lee Milteer,** author of *Spiritual Power Tools for Successful Selling* and *Success Is an Inside Job*

"Alessandra and Teplitz have a winner with their new book, *Switched-On Selling*. Their concept of how to 'rewire' your thinking with new premises, let go of old baggage, and program yourself for more and bigger sales will catapult you to a new level! Don't miss the opportunity to "hard-wire" yourself with these new ideas. Get this book today."

**Don Hutson,** speaker, co-author of the *New York Times* #1 best-seller, *The One Minute Entrepreneur,* and CEO of U.S. Learning

"By combining Jerry's Brain Gym approach with Tony's traditional selling techniques, the knowledge and skills of both speakers and trainers create a powerful synergy in an interactive format that brings the seminar experience to life for the reader. This will be a number one best seller! I look forward to the 'birth' of this book and can't wait to recommend it to all my clients and audiences. Having known Jerry Teplitz and Tony Alessandra for the past 25 years, I can't imagine anyone being more qualified to write *Switched-On Selling*."

**Linda Miles,** CSP, CMC, founder, Linda Miles and Associates and The Speaking Consulting Network, Virginia Beach, VA

"EVERY salesperson needs—and should read—*Switched-On Selling!* In a world filled with sales training similarities, Teplitz and Alessandra have created an approach that gives truly unique and powerful tools to create distinction and success for sales professionals."

**Scott McKain,** author of *Collapse of Distinction* and *What Customers REALLY Want*

"This is a sales book like no other. Instead of the usual book filled with motivation and closing techniques, Teplitz and Alessandra deliver a scientifically based approach that puts you into the mindset needed for sales success. Don't waste any time. It's time to get your brain 'Switched On' and go out and sell!"

**Shep Hyken,** author of *The Cult of the Customer*

"Top sales training professionals Jerry Teplitz and Tony Alessandra have created a radically new way to achieve success by combining their expertise in the novel approach called *Switched-On Selling.* This is a must-read book for anyone in sales. It will have a tremendous impact on your sales ... and your success!"

**Willie Jolley,** radio and television personality and best-selling author of *A Setback Is a Setup for a Comeback* and *Turn Setbacks Into Comebacks!*

"This book is right on target for the modern sales force. It presents a powerful tool called Brain Gym, which provides a scientific approach to switch-on the salesperson's abilities in all aspects of the selling process. This book belongs in every salesperson's and sales manager's library."

**Dave Yoho,** creator of *The Science of Successful Selling* and *Power Linguistics*

"This excellent book shows you how to capture the essence of sales while boosting your bottom line. Teplitz and Alessandra have combined their wealth of experience to create a powerhouse of information."

**Dr. Nido Qubein,** President, High Point University; Chairman, Great Harvest Bread Co.

"Don't just read *Switched-On Selling* ... USE what Teplitz and Alessandra teach in your day-to-day sales work to create your Best Year in sales!"

**Tony Parinello,** author of *Selling to VITO, the Very Important Top Officer*

"Top sales training professionals Teplitz and Alessandra have created a radically new way to achieve success by combining their expertise in the novel approach called **Switched-On Selling**. This is a must-read book for anyone in sales."

**Pam Lontos,** president of PR/PR Public Relations
and author of *I See Your Name Everywhere*

"**Switched-On Selling** provides a valuable, unique and proven approach to getting beyond the unconscious beliefs that get in that way of the success that we desire! Thank you, Jerry and Tony."

**Donna Fisher,** author of *Power Networking, People Power*
and *Professional Networking for Dummies*

"If you've ever suspected that there's more to selling than meets the eye, you are right. My friends and colleagues Jerry Teplitz and Tony Alessandra— both masters of the art of persuasion and influence—will show you ways to eliminate resistance easily and consistently.
So, get up and flip the switch to more sales right now."

**Jim Cathcart,** author of *Relationship Intelligence*®

"The revolutionary approach of **Switched-On Selling** gives salespeople easy tools to immediately switch their brain 'on' for selling success."

**Daniel Burrus,** author of *Technotrends*

"This book is hot! I ought to know, because I wrote the book, *Heat Up Your Cold Calls!* Most sales guides treat just the sales process, without much regard for the people doing the selling ... and the buying. What sets this book apart is its focus on creating a balanced, effective, and healthy salesperson. That's the crucial foundation that all the other books overlook. I've known both authors for decades, and they deliver, consistently."

**George Walther,** author of *Heat Up Your Cold Calls*

# SWITCHED-ON SELLING

## BALANCE YOUR BRAIN
## FOR SALES SUCCESS

# SWITCHED-ON
# SELLING

## BALANCE YOUR BRAIN
## FOR SALES SUCCESS

Jerry V. Teplitz, J.D., Ph.D.
and Tony Alessandra, Ph.D.
with Norma Eckroate

Happiness Unlimited
PUBLICATIONS

Published by Happiness Unlimited Publications
1304 Woodhurst Drive
Virginia Beach, VA 23454


Library of Congress Cataloging-in-Publication Data
Teplitz, Jerry.
    Switched on selling : balance your brain for sales success /
Jerry V. Teplitz, Tony Alessandra, Norma Eckroate.
    p. cm.
    Includes index.
    ISBN 978-0939372-18-8
1. Selling. 2. Success in business. 3. Thought and thinking—Problems, exercises, etc. 4. Intellect—Problems, exercises, etc. 5. Self-actualization (Psychology).
I. Alessandra, Anthony J. II. Eckroate, Norma, 1951-. III. Title.
HF5438.25 .T46 2010
658.85—dc22          2010900417

Printed in the United States of America.

15 14 13 12 11 10 9 8 7 6 5 4 3 2 1


Cover Design by Daniel Yaeger
Book Design by Lynn Snyder
Illustrations by Cris Arbo
Photographs by Elizabeth Balcar
This book is available at quantity discounts for bulk purchases.

For information, please call 800 77-RELAX

**Website: www. Teplitz.com**

# ACKNOWLEDGEMENTS

**Dr. Jerry V. Teplitz:**

I'd like to thank Dr. John Diamond from whom I learned Behavioral Kinesiology, which became a stepping stone to so much of my work. I am also extremely grateful to Dr. Paul Dennison and Gail Dennison, creators of Brain Gym, for their willingness to allow me to use their materials to develop the first version of the Switched-On Selling seminar in 1986 and for their willingness to write and publish the *Brain Gym for Business* book with me.

I am grateful to the late William T. Brooks, CEO of The Brooks Group, who had the vision and willingness to be my initial co-author of this book. And I am thankful to Tony Alessandra for stepping in to fill the void when Bill passed on. Tony, I am grateful that you lent your wisdom and masterful strategies to this collaboration.

This book would simply not have happened if Norma Eckroate had not been willing to become part of it and stick with it over the proverbial bumps in the road. I know my skills and limitations and Norma's skills coincide well by augmenting my limitations. Thank you, Norma!

I am also extremely grateful to Judy Grant, Paula Oleska, and the committees of the Brain Gym® Foundation for their time and effort and for allowing me to use the Brain Gym materials in the book. I also appreciated receiving many of their suggestions which improved the quality of the book. In addition, I'd like to thank Pamela Curlee for her support.

In the production of this book I'd like to thank the following people who played crucial roles: Daniel Yaeger for his wonderful cover artwork; Donna Mosher for her copyediting skills; Lynn Snyder for her masterful layout; Cris Arbo for her great drawings; Beth Agresta and Richard Hagen, and Elizabeth Balcar for their photographs; and Elizabeth Balcar for Photoshopping the photos, which was an enormous job.

And, finally, I am grateful to the subscribers to my Teplitz Email Report who responded to a poll and helped me select the best cover artwork.


**Dr. Tony Alessandra:**
I'd like to especially thank all the people who helped me write and research the sales-related concepts that have improved and enhanced my work over the years: Jim Cathcart for his in-depth self-management content and co-authorship of *The Business of Selling;* Phil Wexler for his pioneering ideas in our *Non-Manipulative Selling* book; Gregg Baron for his customer satisfaction content and co-authorship of our *Sales Professional's Idea-A-Day Guide*; Dr. John Monoky for his sales management materials in our *Sales Manager's Idea-A-Day Guide* book; and Scott Zimmerman for refining my Relationship Strategies materials into *The Platinum Rule Mastery* book series. However, my biggest thanks go to Rick Barrera, my co-author of *Non-Manipulative Selling* and *Collaborative Selling*. Many of the sales ideas in this book come from our work together creating the video-based training program, *The Competitive Advantage*.

In addition, I am also grateful to those who directly and indirectly contributed to my thought processes—Anthony Athos, Warren Bennis, Sheila Murray Bethel, Robert Cialdini, Daniel Goleman, Paul Hersey, Dr. Phil Hunsaker, Alec Mackenzie, Mark McCormack, George Walther, Carl Jung, David Merrill, Dr. Michael O'Connor, Frank Sarr, Ron Finkelstein, Steve Underation, Dale Fetherling, Garry Schaeffer, Larry Wilson, Dr. John Geier, William Moulton Marston, and Myers & Briggs.

# CONTENTS

# INTRODUCTION

Have you ever wondered what it is that sets extraordinary salespeople apart from those who are just getting by? Are they simply more talented or more intelligent? Do they have better connections with decision-makers? Or is something else going on? The fact is that super-successful salespeople not only have great personalities and proven, powerful sales methods, they also have an elusive quality that we might call the X-factor. This X-factor includes inner resilience and a strong ability to empower oneself.

Super-successful salespeople more easily work through challenges and keep focused on their goals. Setbacks are not failures; they are simply temporary obstacles that present new challenges and opportunities. These individuals enjoy their work, they enjoy people, and some of them even seem to enjoy paperwork. Whether they know it or not, they are successful because they have subconscious beliefs that support success.

If you have thoughts like, "Prospects never answer my calls," then it's more likely that your calls will go unanswered. If you believe that closing sales is hard, it will be more difficult to attain success. Any limiting beliefs that you hold about success, abundance, effectiveness or other issues relating to the sales process are part of your subconscious programming. When you are faced with situations relating to these topics, these beliefs automatically kick in.

The big question, though, is this: Where does that programming come from? Why do you automatically "default" to the little voice inside that says that prospects don't respond positively to you? Why doesn't your little inner voice shout out to you: *"I can do this." "Cold calls are easy." "I'm very comfortable and confident when it comes time to ask for the order."*

The problem is that the programming in your subconscious mind is locked in there—like a database of stored programs on a computer.

In his book *Biology of Belief,* Dr. Bruce Lipton explains[1]:

...the subconscious mind is a repository of stimulus-response tapes derived from instincts and learned experiences. The subconscious mind is strictly habitual; it will play the same behavioral responses to life's signals over and over again, much to our chagrin. How many times have you found yourself going ballistic over something trivial like an open toothpaste tube? You have been trained since childhood to carefully replace the cap. When you find the tube with its cap left off, your "buttons are pushed" and you automatically fly into a rage. You've just experienced the simple stimulus-response of a behavior program stored in the subconscious mind.

When it comes to sheer neurological processing abilities, the subconscious mind is millions of times more powerful than the conscious mind. If the desires of the conscious mind conflict with the programs in the subconscious mind, which 'mind' do you think will win over? You can repeat the positive affirmation that you are lovable over and over or that your cancer tumor will shrink. But if, as a child, you heard over and over that you are worthless and sickly, those messages programmed in your subconscious mind will undermine your best conscious efforts to change your life.

Lipton further explains that the *subconscious mind* is like an "autopilot" that processes up to 20,000,000 environmental stimuli per second while the *conscious mind* is a manual control that can process only about forty environmental stimuli per second. Therefore, the subconscious mind, with its speed and efficiency, is basically "autopiloting" our lives. In most cases, those areas of our lives that are successful continue to be successful because our subconscious beliefs support that success. Those areas that are stressful and challenging continue to stress and challenge us because, likewise, we have subconscious beliefs that keep the status quo in place in those areas.

---

1    Lipton, Bruce H., Ph.D., *The Biology of Belief,* Hay House, 2008, pages 97-98.

Many of today's motivational experts explain the same concept in a different way. Some refer to it as the Law of Attraction and tell us that we are attracting everything in our lives, even that which we say "no" to. They say the trick is to focus on what we *want*, not what we *don't want*. However, that's only part of the picture. If will power, commitment, and positive thinking were enough to override limiting beliefs that are programmed in our subconscious, this world would be brimming over with super-successful people.

You may have read many books on selling and attended numerous sales seminars. You might even have a private coach. But the success you're striving for may still be elusive as long as your subconscious mind is running old programming that blocks or limits you. The fact is that most experts don't tell you *how* to change that default setting in your subconscious so it will "default" into positive thinking.

The good news is that there are ways to reprogram the hard drive of our subconscious so we can attain all of the success we want. The "deeper secret" is a brain optimization process that easily reprograms and rebalances that old subconscious programming. *Switched-On Selling* brings together the best of the work of two powerhouse pioneers, Tony Alessandra, Ph.D., and Jerry Teplitz, J.D., Ph.D. We have each dedicated our careers to helping others attain mastery in their lives through our keynotes, seminars, books and coaching. This book combines two very different technologies into an interactive experience that will "switch you on" for sales success.

Dr. Tony Alessandra, a prolific author with eighteen books translated into forty-nine foreign languages, has taught thousands of salespeople how to achieve peak sales performance. Tony's strategies and tips inspire sales professionals and make them feel they were born to be sales leaders.

Dr. Jerry Teplitz, known as "an expert in Brain Performance Optimization," has spent more three decades teaching revolutionary techniques that quite literally switch-on the body and the mind to achieve full potential through optimum brain performance by using movement exercises called Brain Gym®.

What makes Jerry's Switched-On Selling seminar so different, so unique, and so powerful that Tony and other master sales trainers—who have their own training programs—recommend someone else's program so highly? It is because Switched-On Selling is a proven yet revolutionary concept for increasing your bottom-line sales by literally reprogramming your subconscious. This revolutionary brain optimization technique allows you to release old beliefs and programming relating to the sales process. New wiring around your subconscious beliefs will redirect your conscious behavior so you can fully utilize Tony's sales strategies. It gives you tools to easily and quickly empower yourself so that you, too, have the edge in every sales situation.

Switched-On Selling will assist you in fully utilizing the sales techniques you have learned in the past—and it doesn't conflict with any other technique-oriented sales training seminars you learned or trainings you take in the future. As Andy Miller, trainer for the Sandler Training Institute of Virginia, says, "Jerry, you have found the missing piece! This should be a required seminar before anyone pursues traditional sales training."

The Brain Gym, process that you will learn in Switched-On Selling was created by Paul E. Dennison, Ph.D. and Gail E. Dennison[2]. Through a series of movements, exercises, and a process called a Balance, Brain Gym movements will literally reprogram your subconscious beliefs. To use a computer analogy, you will first identify an old belief that isn't serving you. Then you will hit the delete key to release that belief, replace it with a new empowering belief, and, finally, click on "save" to store that new belief permanently in the subconscious mind.

The Brain Gym process that Dr. Teplitz utilizes allows you to easily identify and overcome your fears. Fear has a powerful effect on a person's behavior and can explain the difference between success and failure in sales. When a person is functioning out of fear—for instance, fear of rejection—he will attempt to avoid the cause of the fear. If

---

2    The Brain Gym® movements and exercises used in this publication are used with the permission of Brain Gym International but the application of these movements does not necessarily reflect the educational philosophy of Brain Gym® International or the Brain Gym authors, Paul and Gail Dennison, California, USA.

you are afraid of rejection, you may hesitate to make calls or set up appointments, even with prospects who are interested in your product. As a result, you will not be successful and will have mediocre sales or eventually leave the field altogether.

The Switched-On Selling seminar is so powerful that the prestigious National Association of Sales Professionals officially recognized it as one of their accredited courses. What kind of benefits can you expect from experiencing the Switched-On Selling approach? Jerry has received feedback from numerous attendees about the ways this seminar transformed their lives. Here are a few examples:

Prior to taking the Switched-On Selling seminar, Mike Gegan, a life insurance salesperson from Virginia Beach, Virginia, had not closed a single major contract for three months. Within two weeks after the seminar, he closed eight.

Veda Stone, a life insurance salesperson from Norfolk, Virginia, sold an average of one insurance contract every three weeks. After taking the seminar, her average jumped to two contracts every week—an increase of 500 percent. Veda changed companies nine months after the seminar and, in her first three months at the new company, averaged three contracts a week. And, after only one month with the new company, she was named their top salesperson.

Serge Gravelle, a webmaster from Largo, Florida, said, "The results from taking Jerry's seminar were instantaneous. The day after the seminar, we closed seven contracts, more than in the preceding eight months. By the end of the week, we had eighteen signed contracts."

Sherry Knight, a management consultant in Saskatchewan, Canada, wrote: "Wow! After mastering the techniques you demonstrated in the Switched-On Selling seminar, I made a decision to increase my business income. Jerry, the last year has seen a 50 percent increase in the bottom line. I am thrilled! Anytime a business of fifteen years can grow by 50 percent in just one year, it is remarkable."

Companies who have put their employees through the Switched-On Selling program have experienced dramatic increases in sales, profits, and employee retention. One example is A-Active Termite and Pest Control in Virginia Beach, Virginia. In mid-2009 the company's CEO Kevin Kordek put half his sales force through Jerry's SOS seminar.

Two-and-a-half months later, Kordek reported that one of his sales people had increased his sales 200 percent, overall company sales had gone up around 25 percent, and six of the eight attendees of Switched-On Selling had become top tier performers. And this was in the middle of a recession!

Kordek said, "Since the SOS seminar, our sales increases have been measured by dollars and numbers of new customers. Both are remarkable. I am fascinated by this training, which made it clear to me that subconscious beliefs direct conscious behavior. In addition, the beauty of the training is that students don't even have to understand or recognize the changes in their behavior. They simply follow the steps of the training and then, once trained or 'switched-on,' the results speak for themselves.

"As an employer, I use a different matrix for success from the one that salespeople use. For me, employee retention is a key indicator—and it is also a great measure of employee satisfaction that shows up directly on the bottom line. I'm proud to report that sales/service employee turnover is at a record low and client satisfaction is at an all-time high. The result is efficient, profitable, and sustainable growth! As A-Active grows and adds new people, we will continue to integrate Switched-on-Selling as a part of the orientation training to help ensures new employee success."

Another of Jerry's clients, the South Carolina Farm Bureau, an insurance company, did a research study to determine the effectiveness of the Switched-On Selling seminar. They put one group of their salespeople through the seminar, while a control group did not take the seminar. At the end of four months, the sales figures of both groups were compared with the same four-month period in the previous year. The group that had attended the Switched-On Selling seminar averaged *39 percent higher* sales, while the salespeople who did not take the course had no increase in sales. The seminar participants had even more impressive results in the area of premiums, a revenue stream that is even more important than new sales in the insurance business. Those who took the course increased premiums by *71 percent* over those who didn't take the course.

Jerry also conducted his own study of the effectiveness of the Switched-On Selling seminar on 695 attendees. At the beginning of the seminar, he asked participants to complete an eighteen-item questionnaire that rated their attitudes, perception of themselves and their effectiveness in the selling process. The questionnaire is comprised of a series of statements about the sales process, such as "I handle rejection well" and "I am comfortable with face-to-face visits." The participants were asked to indicate their attitude about each statement, with response choices of "strongly agree," "agree," "disagree," and "strongly disagree." The questionnaire also asked them to rate how well they handle issues such as asking for the order, asking clients for referrals, and making cold calls.

At the end of the seminar, they completed the same questionnaire again to determine the immediate impact of the seminar. A follow up was done a month later when they were asked to complete the questionnaire a third time to determine if the improvement they experienced at the seminar had translated to real-life experience. The follow-up questionnaire was also designed to help determine if the participants had initially overrated the seminar's impact due to the placebo effect or a seminar "high."

The results were remarkable. Here's an example.

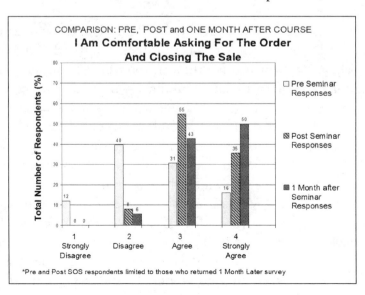

When responding to the statement, *"I am comfortable asking for the order and closing the sale"* at the beginning of the seminar, 52 percent of the participants admitted that asking for the order and closing the sale was a problem for them. Only 16 percent said they handled asking for the order and closing the sale well.

At the end of the seminar, 55 percent of the respondents answered "Well" to asking for the order and closing the sales and 35 percent said "Very Well," while only 8 percent were left saying they still felt it was a problem for them. So during this one-day seminar, something happened to 90 percent of the attendees, who no longer felt uncomfortable asking for the order and closing the sale.

Of course, those responses were given in a vacuum—while the participants were still at the seminar. It was great that they left with the strong feeling that they could now ask for the order and close the sale, but the proof is in the pudding. How would this translate in the real world of daily sales calls? That's why the follow-up questionnaire one month after the seminar was so important. An amazing 50 percent of the individuals who responded to the follow-up questionnaire said they felt they could ask for the order and close the sale very well. This was a jump of 34 percent from the pre-seminar results. Only 6 percent of the respondents still felt it was still a problem for them to ask for the order and close the sale.

A statistician analyzed the results on all the questions and reported that the likelihood of such a rate of improvement was at the .0001 level of probability of occurring. For those of you who are not statisticians, this means the seminar had an extraordinarily beneficial impact on the perceptions of the participants. (Highlights of the study can be found in Appendix B. The full study is available at www.Teplitz.com.)

Jerry conducted another study with people who do sales work for banks. This study indicated that powerful changes occurred for 87 participants from five banks who had attended the one-day Switched-On Selling seminar (SOS). In the study, one of the statements was "It is easy for me to ask clients for referrals." At the beginning of the seminar day 54 percent of the attendees said that asking for referrals was difficult or very difficult for them while at the end of the day only 12 percent still felt that way. And a month later only 8 percent still had a negative experience with asking for referrals. (The complete study can be found at www.Teplitz.com.)

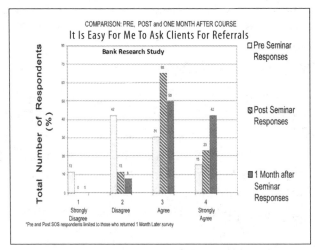

These studies show that the seminar empowered participants in numerous aspects of the sales process, including handling rejection and asking for referrals, while releasing fears, worries, and concerns. Almost everyone who participated became switched-on to the sales process, yet they did it without learning a single new sales technique.

What made these remarkable results possible? These individuals simply attended the Switched-On Selling seminar, participated in the process, and walked out "switched-on" for selling. This book takes you through the same information and processes that Dr. Teplitz presents in the SOS Seminar. In this book, you've got it all. Jerry's mind-body re-wiring approach is matched with the techniques and strategies of Tony Alessandra, who is one of the world's foremost sales gurus, giving you tools to reach levels of success that you may not have thought possible.

Just like seminar participants, when you complete this book, you will find that:

• What you are already doing, you will do even better;
• What you would like to do better, you will easily improve; and
• What you are avoiding doing, you will be able to do.

Switched-On Selling is about changing your mind. Literally. If you have ever felt insecure before a meeting with a new potential prospect, or decided to clean your desk instead of making cold calls, or felt ineffective during a sales presentation, be prepared for some life-changing synergy as you learn how to re-educate your brain using your body with the Brain Gym movements and, at the same time, integrate the expertise of Tony's proven sales techniques and strategies.

## A Few Words from Tony

Switched-On Selling offers a unique combination of solid sales skills and strategies coupled with the exciting breakthrough of the Brain Gym movements, creating a unique, one-of-a-kind experience for any reader. Think about it ... there is no other, singular approach anywhere in the world that offers this dual track for sales people in such a meaningful and powerful way— my approach to selling and Jerry's approach to balancing your brain present a unique approach for selling success.

## A Few Words from Jerry

In this book you will learn a process called Brain Gym, which easily enables you to remove the mental blocks you experience in any part of the selling process. This process allows you to re-format your mental programming and activate new neural pathways so you can balance your brain in new ways.

Did you know that the stem cells in your body manufacture 10,000 new brain cells every day? Scientists use the term neuroplasticity to describe the ability of the brain to develop new neuronal and synaptic connections and thereby re-wire itself. It was once believed that only children's brains had this capacity but now we know that adult's brains can also be re-wired or redeveloped. And that's what we're doing with Brain Gym. Through a series of easy movements and exercises, you can simply and easily re-wire and create new balance in the circuitry of your brain to generate these new neural pathways to enhance performance in all areas of your life, including intellectual, creative, athletic, and interpersonal, and of course, in the case of this book, selling. As I mentioned earlier, it's as if you are clicking on "delete" to release the old belief, hitting "replace" to install the new belief, and then clicking "save" to store that new belief. And you wind up with a new balance in your brain.

Switched-On Selling utilizes this brain optimization technology for all of the aspects of the sales process, including goal setting, pre-approach, prospecting, presentation, follow-up, and prosperity. For example, let's look at cold calling. Since you never know if the person you plan to cold call will be receptive, indifferent, or even hostile to your call, it can be difficult to get up the nerve to place the call in the first place. Some salespeople even react with a sense of relief when they get a prospect's voice mail and can just leave a message instead of talking to the person. A salesperson who dislikes cold calling may put off calling by finding other things to do, such as cleaning the desk, closet, or car. For these people, *anything* is better than the possibility of being rejected.

The stress of having to make cold calls can be debilitating and, if it's a key element of their jobs, some people will quit because they can never get up the nerve to pick up the phone. Others find a self-fulfilling prophecy occurs when they finally talk to the prospect and the call goes so badly that it confirms for them that they shouldn't have bothered to attempt the call in the first place. In many sales positions, the ability to successfully make cold calls can be the difference between succeeding or failing.

The brain integration techniques in Switched-On Selling will allow you to immediately move past these kinds of blocks as well as all other mental and/or physical blocks that you might have in the selling process. Once you have gone through this process, your brain will be switched-on—and that will allow you to fully incorporate and utilize Tony's sales strategies. This combination of leading-edge mind-body technology with leading-edge sales strategies gives you everything you need to be the most effective and successful salesperson possible.

From my own research studies, the research that our corporate clients have done, and the stories that graduates of the SOS Seminar have shared, I can say with total confidence that the Switched-On Selling course works and that you can change your professional life through this amazing system.

## Our Challenge to You

For the sales professional with some experience, we know you've put lots of time and effort into your craft. We're not suggesting that you start over. But we are suggesting that you re-wire and rebalance your brain's programming to more fully utilize and optimize what you have learned in the past by using this book as an interactive tool. Perhaps you feel you've really mastered some arenas of Tony's sales strategies. While you have the choice of skipping ahead to another section of the book, we're suggesting that you don't do that. If you are very experienced in sales, then the best way to use this book is to look at it as a refresher course. The tools Jerry presents using Brain Gym give you the opportunity to stop while you're reading and literally jump into "re-wiring and rebalancing mode," just as if you were at one of his live presentations.

If you are new to sales, this book will get you over your blocks even before you experience them. As you learn the techniques of how to sell, you'll simply be saying to yourself, "I can do that," "That's a piece of cake," "That's easy." Like others who have used this simple tool, you will quickly move to seeing immediate demonstrations of success where it counts—in your real world experiences.

As you do the exercises in this book, you will need to actively participate in order to go beyond your intellectual understanding of sales strategies. Switched-On Selling is not about having an intellectual understanding of something; it is about re-wiring and rebalancing your brain to release the mental and physical blockages that are holding you back from the level of success you desire.

Here's how the book is divided:

- In Part I, Jerry explains Brain Gym and how it is used in Switched-On Selling. He also presents descriptions and explanations of all of the Brain Gym Movements and Exercises that you will perform in the Balances in Part II.
- Part II is divided into the various aspects of the selling process— goal setting, enjoying selling, planning, prospecting, presentation, follow-up, and prosperity. In each of these chapters, Tony shares

sales success strategies. Then, at the end of each chapter, Jerry takes you through the Brain Gym process, ending with a Balance[3] to switch you on for the aspects of the sales process that you specifically need to improve. If you are doing an aspect of the selling process and would like to improve it, Switched-On Selling will allow you to become even more effective and successful.

- In Part III, Jerry will show you how to continue to reinforce the rebalancing you have done and how to set your energy and focus every day by using the Brain Gym movements and exercises.

So sit back, relax, and participate, as you are now about to experience the life-changing power of Switched-On Selling. Enjoy the journey!

---

3   The Switched-On Selling Balances are designed differently from the way Brain Gym Balances are taught in the Brain Gym Courses.

# PART I

Brain Optimization™—Re-Wiring
& Rebalancing Your Brain
for Sales Success

BY JERRY V. TEPLITZ, J.D., PH.D.

# CHAPTER 1

# WHAT IS BRAIN OPTIMIZATION?

In the Switched-On Selling seminar, a process called Brain Gym literally optimizes your mind-body system by re-educating it and rebalancing it so you can accomplish any skill or function with greater ease and efficiency. Specific Brain Gym movements and exercises are used to activate different parts of the brain for optimal storage, retrieval, and processing of information. The goal is to integrate the whole brain for optimal functioning by reprogramming any areas in which your beliefs are blocking the achievement of your goals.

Brain Gym was originally developed by Dr. Paul Dennison, an educator and researcher who originally worked with children and adults with learning challenges and/or difficulties with motor coordination skills. Dr. Dennison discovered that these problems were caused by a lack of coordination among the different parts of the brain; therefore, he sought innovative ways to use the mind-body connection to help these individuals learn.

After fifteen years of research, Dr. Dennison combined the techniques used in Applied Kinesiology and Neural Optometry, as well as research in the fields of movement, education and child development theory, into a unique system of learning and brain re-patterning that creates new neural wiring in the brain. As his work continued, Dr. Dennison also developed methods to integrate other parts of the brain for a "whole brain" integration that includes the left and right hemispheres, the top and bottom, and the front and back of the brain. Dr. Dennison began this work in 1969 and today thousands of practitioners and instructors facilitate Brain Gym programs in classrooms, businesses, and homes around the world.

In case you read that last paragraph quickly, let me restate the one idea that is of primary importance to an understanding of Brain

Gym—it is designed to integrate the different parts of the brain. *It does this by creating new neural wiring in the brain, which rebalances the brain for optimum success.* In this book, you will frequently see the words "re-wiring" and "re-educating" and "rebalancing." This is literally what Brain Gym does. It allows you to release old thought patterns that negatively impact the way you function in the world and re-wire the neural pathways to allow for re-education and rebalancing. This process creates new reactions and new pathways in a positive vein. If this sounds like a big claim, you'll have the opportunity to read the research and experience it for yourself as you do the exercises. So read on. Let the evidence and your experience of your own re-educated neural wiring become the real proof of the power of this work.

I first became aware of Brain Gym one day while I was waiting for a flight in an airport after teaching a seminar. A man introduced himself to me and said that he had been at one of my business seminars several years earlier and found the material I presented called Behavioral Kinesiology very impactful. He told me that my seminar opened him up to further explorations and he was now studying a new method of brain integration called Brain Gym. He showed me how to do some of the movements involved with this process and I was immediately impressed. The process made my body feel relaxed in the midst of a bustling airport and I even had an appreciable energy boost. I was interested!

At the time, Brain Gym was taught under the banner of Educational Kinesiology, also known as "Edu-K." I signed up for the first three-day Edu-K[4] class  and quickly realized the profound implication of the process when applied to business. As I mentioned, the Brain Gym movements were originally developed to assist those with learning challenges. However, in the past few decades Brain Gym has been adapted to many other arenas for both children and adults, including regular classroom settings where it has led to significant improvements for students in subjects such as reading, spelling, math, handwriting, and

---

4    Information on Brain Gym classes can be obtained by contacting Brain Gym International at www.braingym.org.

test-taking. Students who use Brain Gym movements also experience improvements in comprehension, concentration, communication, memory, organizational skills, performance skills, and overcoming hyperactivity

Brain Gym movements and exercises bring neurological efficiency to your brain, enhancing your body's innate intelligence and quickly replacing old patterns of negative reactions and emotions with positive emotions and responses. This is the key—this system not only makes your brain more efficient, it also allows you to get rid of negative programming.

As a result of improved performance, Brain Gym also leads to greater self-esteem and self-confidence. This may sound like a big claim, but you'll have the opportunity to experience it for yourself as you release old thought patterns that negatively impact the way you function as a salesperson. So read on. Let the evidence and the experience of your own re-education and rebalancing becomes the real proof of the power of this work.

Carla Hannaford, author of *Smart Moves: Why Learning is Not All in Your Head,* states that Brain Gym, as well as other movements like walking, dancing, skipping, twirling, Tai Chi, Yoga, and even the rough and tumble play of children appear to cause adjustments that assist the brain in the learning process. Dee Coulter, a cognitive specialist and neuroscience educator quoted in Hannaford's book, calls these adjustments "micro-interventions." She explains that these adjustments bring about major change because they supply the necessary integration and also reverse the expectation of failure.[5]

Brain Gym simply enhances the body's abilities to do what it does naturally. These movements and exercises can create the opportunity for greater selling success than you have ever imagined and they can also be used to enhance memory, learning, physical coordination, and the achievement of your life goals.

I saw applications for this work in the business world and received permission to expand Brain Gym in that direction by creating the

---

5   Hannaford, Carla. *Smart Moves: Why Learning Is Not All In Your Head.* 1995. Salt Lake City, Utah: Great River Books, 2005, page 110.

Switched-On Selling seminar, which I started teaching in 1986. I also coauthored the book *Brain Gym for Business* with Dr. Paul Dennison and Gail Dennison.

## Why the Brain Switches Off

Your brain is filled with patterns and programming that are "locked" in. These patterns and programs control your thoughts, your reactions, your interactions with others, your ability to effectively apply sales techniques, and even your ability to be spontaneous. If this programming has negative messages locked in, then no matter how many sales techniques you learn or how naturally gifted you may be, your success may be difficult and limited.

The programming that is locked into your brain comes from many sources, including your DNA. It is also has developed from the four pillars of your youth—your parents, your peers, your school, and your culture. If you were repeatedly exposed to the idea that you weren't "good" enough or smart enough; that only "lucky" people are successful; that your sex, the color of your skin, your ethnic background, or your height, weight, or age restrict your chances in life; or any one of thousands of other negative, self-limiting beliefs, you have probably incorporated those beliefs into your life and are unconsciously living out those messages every day. Most people aren't even consciously aware of the extent to which limited thinking is wired into their brain. In many cases, these messages feed your "self talk"—the chatter that goes on in your head—constantly reinforcing the "I'm not good enough" messages. All you need to do is look at your life to know if that is the case for you. Simply ask yourself: *Do I have what I want—or does success seem elusive?*

When your brain is "switched-off" to certain aspects of the sales process, it is a struggle to perform them. As I mentioned earlier, a salesperson may be about to make cold calls and then suddenly decide instead to clean the desk or organize the files—anything to avoid making the cold call. Another example is a salesperson on a sales visit to a new prospect who does a great job of developing rapport and probing the prospect, but doesn't close the sale because she is afraid to ask for the order. In these cases, the idea of making the cold call or asking for the order is switching off the salesperson's brain. And when the brain switches off, it becomes such a struggle to perform the task at hand that the easiest thing to do is to avoid it by doing something else or doing it poorly.

The brain can also switch off to certain activities due to a built-in survival mechanism. To understand how this works, we have to look at the amygdala, a part of the brain that we inherited from our primitive ancestors. Located deep within the medial temporal lobes of the brain, these almond-shaped groups of neurons perform a primary role in the memory as it relates to processing emotional reactions. The amygdala is triggered whenever a threatening situation arises, initiating the "fight, freeze, or flight" response in the body and basically overriding the "rational" part of the brain.

Psychologist Daniel Goleman refers to the amygdala as "the specialist for emotional matters."[6] In his book, *Emotional Intelligence,* Goleman explains that it is this area of the brain that gauges the emotional significance of events. He shares the story of a young man whose amygdala was surgically removed to control seizures. After the surgery, the young man became totally disinterested in people and preferred no human contact. With no amygdala, he seemed to have no feelings at all.

The amygdala is wired to analyze every experience we have to determine if trouble looms. Goleman explains[7]:

> This puts the amygdala in a powerful post in mental life, something like a psychological sentinel, challenging every situation, every perception, with but one kind of question in mind, the most primitive: "Is this something I hate? That hurts me? Something I fear?" If so—if the external event that you are experiencing draws a "Yes"—the amygdala reacts instantaneously, like a neural tripwire, telegraphing a message of crisis to all parts of the brain. In the brain's architecture, the amygdala is poised something like an alarm company where

---

6    Goleman, Daniel, Ph.D., *Emotional Intelligence,* Bantam Books, 1995, page 15.
7    Goleman, page 16.

operators stand ready to send out emergency calls to the fire department, police, and a neighbor whenever a home security system signals trouble. When it sounds an alarm of say, fear, it sends urgent messages to every major part of the brain: it triggers the secretion of the body's fight-or-flight hormones, which mobilizes the centers for movement, and activates the cardiovascular system, the muscles, and the gut.

To the extent that the amygdala takes over during an emotional emergency, the rational part of the brain doesn't have a chance to control what's going on. This rational part, which governs choice, is in the part of the brain called the cerebrum, which developed much later in the evolution of the human brain. An example of the amygdala-in-action is a news story about an out-of-control van that careened into three women pedestrians, striking all three. A number of bystanders reacted by rushing to the van, pulling the driver and passenger from their vehicle, and beating them to death. Seven men were charged with the murder of the driver and his passenger. It turned out that the accident was not even due to driver error. Of course, whether the driver was in error or not, the mob reaction had no justification. This type of deadly group reaction can be the result of emotional hijacking of the brain by the portion of the amygdala that triggered the adrenaline response. There are numerous news stories of people reacting first, thinking second. The amygdala takes charge and otherwise-sane people sometimes respond insanely.

So how can we control which part of the brain is in charge? Let's look at a common activity that is difficult for some people, such as driving on the freeway, and see how the brain processes the information. A person who is challenged by freeway driving doesn't even have to be behind the wheel to have a reaction to it. All he has to do is *think* about driving on the freeway for his brain to be triggered. As soon as the brain is presented with the thought of freeway driving, it quickly reviews the situation to determine if there are any past situations that relate to this thought. Keep in mind that we're talking about a *thought* and not the actual act of driving on the freeway. The situation from the past may be a time in his childhood when he was in an accident or saw an accident on the freeway. The fear feeling he has now about driving on freeways is caused by this past event "kicking in." He doesn't have a choice about how to act in the matter because situations in his past have wired his emotional circuitry to respond with fear. He is switched off to freeway driving.

Fear is a powerful force that can stop us from achieving what we want. Thoughts that a salesperson might have such as "What if I can't succeed at it?" "What if I get rejected?" and "What will people say?" may be occurring at both the conscious and unconscious level. These fears will keep you stuck as they influence your thoughts, attitudes, and even the level of enthusiasm you project as a salesperson. The Brain Gym movements can eliminate and release these fears and, at the same time, re-educate the brain and body to prefer a positive pattern so you are able to achieve the success you desire.

## Brain Gym in Other Arenas

As explained earlier, Brain Gym can be used in many different areas of our personal life and work life, including education and sports. The success of the Switched-On Selling seminar led me to develop an additional seminar for managers called Switched-On Management and one for network marketers called Switched-On Network Marketing.

In addition to creating those seminars, I assisted Pamela Curlee in the creation of her original manual for a golf seminar called Switched-On Golf"®. Pamela's physician husband, Paul, was a mediocre golfer before taking the seminar. Afterwards he became the proud winner of four golf tournaments and dropped his handicap from 18 to 10.

Another Switched-On Golf attendee was a golf instructor who reported that the first time he played after taking the seminar he hit a hole-in-one. Impressed by his own success with Brain Gym, he incorporated the Brain Gym movements into his students' golf lessons. In the first summer that he did this, three of his thirty students hit holes-in-one! Ask any golfer and they'll tell you these numbers are simply amazing.

In addition to helping Pamela create the original Switched-On Golf seminar, I've also created a DVD called *Par and Beyond: Secrets to Better Golf* that demonstrates many more brain integration methods that I've learned and developed from Behavioral Kinesiology. A typical response to this DVD is contained in a letter I received from Shep Hyken after he put the methods into practice. He writes:

> Within a week of watching the video my scores started dropping two to four strokes each round. I was finding that my drives were going longer and more in play than usual … I was a 16 handicap just a month ago. I've been hovering around 15-16 for the last several years. Since watching the program, I've dropped to a 14 and according to the computer I'm trending to a 12! And I don't even practice! More pars seem to be the norm. And just ten days ago I shot the best round ever at my home course—a 76! Your video program allows me to concentrate and focus like I've never done before… It works!"

Here's another response. This one is from Tom Fox, writer for *Travel and Leisure Golf* magazine:

> I was ready to throw my clubs in the nearest water hazard because the game had stopped being fun for me. It's easy to obsess about swing thoughts and mental checklists, which are all about what to think about. *Par and Beyond* focuses on *how* to think and the difference shows up on the scorecard and in congratulations from your playing partners. Jerry's techniques improved my game, but more important, reminded me how to have fun playing a game I love.

Another testimonial came from Ed Hipp, who was selected Golf Coach of the Year of Iowa High Schools, who feels so positive about the impact of *Par and Beyond* that he has endorsed it and recommends it to his clients.

For more information, visit my website at www.Golf-Help.info.

## The Brain Switch:
## Balancing the Brain's Hemispheres

To understand Brain Gym, we need to briefly explore the way the brain works so you'll see how it applies to the selling process. It's important to note that, for the purposes of this book, I am presenting a rather simplified model of brain functioning by focusing on the left hemisphere and right hemispheres of the cerebral cortex. Although science now concludes that there are no absolutes when it comes to brain organization, generally we think of the left brain as the logical, analytical side of the brain and the right brain as the gestalt or the "big picture" part of the brain.

Let's start with the *left hemisphere* which, besides being the logical hemisphere, takes the lead for skills such as language and arithmetic. It processes information piece by piece, logically, analytically, and in a sequential manner. The left hemisphere also generally controls physical movement of the right side of our body. The *right hemisphere* is primarily the reflex or gestalt hemisphere. It has the ability to see the whole picture rather than focusing on the individual pieces. It is the receptive side of the brain and it absorbs and stores information gathered by the senses. The right hemisphere also controls physical movement of the left side of our body.

When the two hemispheres are integrated and balanced, they cooperate and communicate with each other, giving us the ability to function smoothly in our daily lives. This is constantly happening as messages from the body are transmitted as electrical and chemical signals through the nervous system, the circulatory system to the brain, and then back to the body. For example, when you want to turn on a light switch, you first have the thought that the light is off and needs to be turned on. To accomplish this task you walk across the room, raise your hand to the switch, and flip the switch with your fingers. A coordination of movements in both the left and right hemispheres is necessary for even this simple action to be carried out. If your hemispheres weren't integrated and communicating, you might end up stumbling over a piece of furniture, putting a hole in the wall, or going out the door instead of turning on the light.

So how does this relate to the world of sales? A lack of brain coordination can result in a host of difficulties and challenges, such as:
- Difficulty making cold calls
- Difficulty remembering product features and benefits
- Struggling to write a sales letter

- Problems comprehending written material or technical specifications about your products
- Recording your appointments on the wrong date in your calendar
- Reluctance to record notes from sales calls
- Difficulty focusing on the discussion in a sales meeting
- Challenges in keeping your files and records in order
- Difficulty answering questions or objections

When you function primarily out of just the left or the right side of the brain you are functioning "homolaterally," which means one-sided functioning. An example of what this means is found in our school systems. The education system in this country features an analytic approach, causing an over-emphasis on left hemisphere dominance. To succeed in this learning environment, students need to focus on being more left-brain dominant because most of their daily tasks do not involve the right hemisphere. The result is that children who are predominately right hemisphere wired struggle to succeed.

The left and right hemispheres of the brain communicate with each other via the corpus callosum, the membrane that divides the two hemispheres. In a baby, there are 200 million nerve fibers that run across the corpus callosum connecting both hemispheres. It can be compared to a superhighway that allows messages to go back and forth between the two hemispheres, sending reactions and thoughts in the form of electrochemical impulses. The brain contains an estimated one quadrillion nerve connections. But as we get older and continually emphasize one hemisphere over the other, many of these connections begin to atrophy. Therefore, as most people age, there are fewer connections available, which means fewer messages are going across the corpus callosum. This makes it even more challenging to use the "whole" brain and we end up with a "one-brained" or homolateral approach to life, with only one side of the brain firing at a time. For this reason, performing right-hemispheric functions, as well as functions that require both hemispheres to operate together, is more difficult for many people.

The learning challenges that result cause us to develop compensating mechanisms to survive in the world. For example, a student might instinctively begin to sit on the far left side of a classroom because he can better understand what is being written on the chalkboard or comprehend what the teacher is saying from the left side of the room. Even though he is not aware of the reasons behind it, he has found this is a way to compensate for the lack of his brain's integration. These compensating mechanisms allow the person to perform an activity with greater success, but there is a price to pay because it is still generally more difficult and takes longer to do the task. And that is especially true if he has no choice but to sit on the "wrong" side of the room. While the learning challenges faced by the average person aren't as exaggerated as those with attention deficit disorder or dyslexia, they do have an impact on the way we function and on our success in the world.

Over 10,000 brain cells are manufactured in your body every single day. And these brain cells have a built-in "plasticity," or ability to evolve. Brain Gym allows us to utilize this neuroplasticity and stimulate the brain creating more branching neural pathways. But when brain stimulation stops, so does the branching. According to Carla Hannaford[8]:

"These pathways alter from moment to moment in our lives. Ultimately they form only a few permanent connections at the synapses with particular target cells. Experience can further modify these synapses as well. Many synaptic connections are made as new learning occurs. Later, these linkages are pared down in a specific way that increases efficiency of thought. Neurons may have anywhere from 1,000 to 10,000 synapses and may receive information from 1,000 other neurons. Neurons with the most connections, an average of 300,000, are located in the cerebellum, the primary movement center of the brain, again pointing to the importance of movement and experience to learning."

---

8   Hannaford, page 24.

Brain Gym gives us the ability to release old patterns so we can learn with less stress and develop more confidence. It enhances our ability to access our natural creativity by using more of our mental and physical potential. The movements also assist in clearing emotional stress that can affect us both mentally and physically. Reported benefits include improvements in such areas as vision, listening, learning, memory, self-expression, and coordination in children and adults. Teachers typically report improvements in attitude, attention, discipline, behavior, test-taking and homework performance for all participants in the classroom. As a salesperson, when you experience a part of the selling process that you have difficulty with—for example, answering questions, asking for the order, or handling objections—it may almost feel as if you have a disability in that specific part of the selling process. The Brain Gym Balances, movements, and exercises in this book will allow you to immediately change your outcomes and improve your abilities and your successes.

## The Elements of Brain Gym

The main focus of Brain Gym is a process called the Balance. The Brain Gym process balances the brain and the body for specific tasks or goals by releasing past blockages or present difficulties and then re-educating the brain to allow for positive choices and actions. In this book, I've created specific Balances, each of which is focused on an aspect of the selling process. For example, if you are having difficulty placing cold calls, you will do a Balance for Prospecting. This Balance will switch you on to more easily and effectively make cold calls.

However, before you do the Balance, there are several other components that are used in the process. They are:

- **Internal Biofeedback Responses:** You will learn to obtain responses from your mind-body connection using *one* of several different methods:
  1. Noticing
  2. Self Muscle Checking
  3. Muscle Checking with a Partner

Noticing and Self Muscle Checking are done by yourself, while a partner is necessary for Muscle Checking with a Partner. All of these biofeedback response methods will give you feedback to let you know when your body is switched-on by a stimuli and when it is switched off. You will also learn how to get "yes" and "no" responses from your body's own innate intelligence.

- **Brain Gym Movements and Exercises:** As discussed earlier, these movements and exercises are simple positions, exercises, or movements that re-wire the neural pathways in the brain for the goals you desire.
- **Calibration**[9]**:** This process is a series of steps, including Brain Gym movements and exercises that prepare a person for learning. Calibration is also done before beginning Noticing, Self Muscle Checking, or Muscle Checking with a Partner to confirm that the responses you are getting are accurate and that your mind and body are in a state of being ready to learn.

In the next chapter, we'll discuss and explain your Internal Biofeedback Responses.

---

9   The protocol for Calibration is a variation of PACE, as it is taught in other Brain Gym classes.

# CHAPTER 2

# INTERNAL BIOFEEDBACK RESPONSES

Internal biofeedback responses are "answers" you receive from your own body. The goal is to collect data and information about the ways in which your mind and your body respond to specific stimuli. In order to do the Brain Gym processes, you'll first need to determine which method of biofeedback response works best for you. You'll learn this when you get to Chapter 3. But first let's look at the history of internal biofeedback response methods and why these methods work.

## The History of Biofeedback Responses

The system of biofeedback response used in this book, which I refer to as muscle checking, was developed by Dr. John Diamond in the late 1970s. Dr. Diamond was a psychiatrist who had become frustrated in his practice. During treatment, many of his patients would initially get better but, when they returned to the conditions that had caused or aggravated their problems in the first place, they would often backslide. Dr. Diamond searched for a way to identify their physical, nutritional, and emotional needs to help them achieve more long-lasting wellness. But despite all of his attempts, the conditions that caused his patients' psychological problems often eluded him. Dr. Diamond was on a mission to determine the specific triggers that were contributing to their illnesses so he could help eliminate them.

Dr. Diamond finally found an answer in the principles of a healing system called Applied Kinesiology and the decades-old system of muscle checking that is employed in Applied Kinesiology. Utilizing the muscle checking techniques he learned, his research showed that the body is instantly switched off when it is impacted by negative emotional issues or mental stresses. He realized then that muscle checking could be used to diagnose and treat emotional and mental health problems because it enabled him to isolate a patient's problems and therefore better understand its root causes. Once these specific stresses were identified, he was better able to assist his patients in finding ways to alter these stresses. Consequently, his patients got well faster and had fewer relapses.

Dr. Diamond developed a system called Behavioral Kinesiology (BK) and found it to be an easy and accurate way to get information from the body's own innate intelligence. This system is used to "ask" the body what switches it on and what switches it off, as well as to obtain "yes" and "no" responses to questions.

Muscle checking allows you to determine exactly what forces, both external and internal, are stressful to your body. Then, once you identify the negative stresses in your life, you can focus on reducing, changing or eliminating them. In this book you'll learn that the more stresses and negative programming that you eliminate from your life, the more energy and ability you will have available to accomplish what you want. You can read more about Dr. Diamond's breakthrough work in his books, *Your Body Doesn't Lie* (also published under the title *BK: Behavioral Kinesiology*) and *Life Energy* and in Jerry's book, *Switched-On Living.*

While this book focuses on your sales goals, the bottom line is that every aspect of your life will benefit. Muscle checking can even be used to determine which elements of your environment switch you on and which elements switch you off. This includes the type of lighting used in your home or office, the color of your walls, and the music you listen to.

Dr. Diamond's muscle checking research has also demonstrated that there are many other factors that have either beneficial or adverse effects on the body's life energy. They include facial and bodily expressions, music, art, and graphics, and even modulations of the voice and emotions. He found that these reactions are almost universal—almost everyone has the same response to specific stimuli. These responses are not due to a person's beliefs, reasoning ability, or logic. For example, a smile universally switches people on, while a frown universally switches people off. Images of negative news events are weakening. These results are consistent no matter what background or culture the person being muscle checked comes from.

As I mentioned, Dr. Diamond developed Behavioral Kinesiology after studying the principles of Applied Kinesiology. Applied Kinesiology was developed in 1964 by a chiropractor, Dr. George Goodheart. It is a diagnostic and treatment system that incorporates muscle checking as an augment to medical examination and treatment procedures. It is used by doctors of chiropractic, osteopathy, homeopathy, dentistry, and medicine as well as by other trained professionals in the field of kinesiology.

Historically, however, muscle checking, which is also referred to as kinesiology, goes even further back in the medical annals. It was first discovered and developed as a system for diagnosis and treatment in 1912 by Dr. Robert Lovett of Harvard Medical School. Dr. Lovett, a professor of orthopedic surgery, first discovered the isolated muscle test in his work with paralyzed children. His goal was to measure the degree of muscle function in the partially or completely paralyzed little bodies of his patients. Referred to by Dr. Lovett as a "gravity test," a muscle associated with joint movement was positioned so that it was isolated and then tugged or pushed while the patient resisted. The degree to which the patient was able to resist determined the degree of integrity in the muscle. Thus, by isolating and testing muscles, a sensitive and individually specific means to determine muscle strength or weakness became available.

Dr. Charles Lowman, an orthopedic surgeon took this concept further. Then, in 1936, physical therapists Henry and Florence Kendall researched and wrote copiously about the use of the isolated muscle test for the purpose of determining muscle strength or weakness. In 1949, they published a book called *Muscles: Testing and Function* in 1949. Florence Kendall had impressive credentials: She was a consultant to the Surgeon General of the United States, a member of the Maryland State Board of Physical Therapy Examiners, a faculty member in the University of Maryland School of Medicine, and an instructor in Body Mechanics at Johns Hopkins Hospital.

Despite its proven efficacy, muscle checking was, to a great extent, "lost" with the beginning of World War II. By necessity, medical doctors moved into battlefield medicine, consisting mostly of surgery and drugs. Then, in 1964, Dr. George Goodheart rediscovered muscle checking and re-introduced it to the medical world through the diagnostic treatment modality he called Applied Kinesiology.

The next big leap in application came in 1981 with the work of Dr. Paul Dennison and Gail Dennison and their use of muscle checking as part of their Brain Gym processes.

## Why Muscle Checking Works

Researchers believe that muscle checking works because of alterations in the functioning of the nervous system, leading to muscle strength or weakness. Muscle weakness can be attributed to various causes such as the blockage of an acupuncture meridian line, a chemical imbalance, or even a disturbing thought pattern.

Dr. David Hawkins, a psychiatrist, has been at the forefront of research on mental processes for decades. In the early 1970s, when the medical profession was resistant, even hostile, to the fact that nutrition has an impact on physical and mental health, Dr. Hawkins co-authored a book on that subject, *Orthomolecular Psychiatry*, with two-time Nobel Laureate Dr. Linus Pauling. Now a leading researcher on muscle checking, Dr. Hawkins explains the reasons it works in his book *Power Vs. Force*[10]:

> Each of us possesses a computer far more advanced than the most elaborate artificial intelligence machine available, one that's available at any time—the human mind itself. The basic function of any measuring device is simply to give a signal indicating the detection by the instrument of slight change ... The reactions of the human body provide such a signal of change in conditions. As will be seen, the body can discern, to the finest degree, the difference between that which is supportive of life and that which is not. This isn't surprising: After all, living things react positively to what is life-supportive and negatively to what is not; this is a fundamental mechanism of survival.

Another study that validates muscle checking as a diagnostic tool was done with 89 college students and published in *Perceptual and Motor Skills*[11]. The purpose of the study was to determine if a muscle is switched off when a person makes a false statement and if it remains switched on when the person makes a true statement. The study

---

10 Hawkins, David, M.D., Ph.D., *Power Vs. Force: The Hidden Determinants of Human Behavior,* Hay House, Inc. 2002 (Revised Edition), page 44.
11 Muscle Test Comparisons of Congruent and Incongruent Self-Referential Statements by Daniel Monti, M.D., John Sinnott, Marc Marchese, Elisabeth J. S. Kunkel, Jeffrey M. Greeson, published in *Perceptual and Motor Skills,* 1999 (88, 1019-1028).

participants were asked to repeat four statements, two that were true and two that were false, and they were muscle checked after making each of the statements. They were asked to say, "My name is" and then state their real name. Then they were asked to say, "My name is" and say a name that was not theirs. They were also asked to say, "I am an American citizen" and "I am a Russian citizen." (All of the students selected for the study were American citizens.) The students were randomly assigned the order in which they were to make these statements. They did not know the purpose of the study, nor were any of them familiar with muscle checking.

The muscle checking was performed with sophisticated equipment that measured a combination of the pressure being applied by the person doing the muscle checking and the resistance of the muscle of the person being checked. The muscle checking was done by asking each participant to raise one arm out to their side and then resist while the other person pushed down on it. The researchers were looking at the variables of how long the person was able to keep the arm up and the amount of force that was necessary to push the arm down. The testing method differed from normal muscle checking in that the testers were pushing to the arm's fatigue level so that even on the strengthening statements the arm would eventually come down, but it took much more time and pressure to get it down. On false statements, they were able to push the arm down an average of 58.9 percent faster and the amount of force used was an average of 17.2 percent less pressure than on the true statements. The results of this study showed scientifically significant validation that muscle checking is highly accurate.

Today, the effectiveness of muscle checking is clear to the thousands and thousands of people who use it on a regular basis. The applications and uses for muscle checking have proliferated over the years into many different methods that have been developed by researchers and health professionals. Here are some of the organizations and individuals who use or promote muscle checking:

- Dr. Goodheart established the International College of Applied Kinesiology, which publishes a research journal. Today many chiropractors use Applied Kinesiology in their practice. (See www.icak.com)

- Dr. John Thie, a chiropractor, developed Touch for Health, which is the layperson's version of Applied Kinesiology. (See www.tfhka.org)
- Neuro Emotional Technique (NET.), a method of chiropractic developed by Dr. Scott Walker, incorporates muscle checking to determine the emotional components of health problems. (See www.netmindbody.com)
- Nambudripad's Allergy Elimination Technique (NAET) was developed by Dr. Devi S. Nambudripad, a chiropractor and acupuncturist. As the name of this system implies, it is used to eliminate allergies. (See www.naet.com)
- Emotional Freedom Techniques (EFT), created by Gary Craig, uses muscle checking as an optional method of diagnosis in a process that clears emotional blocks. (See www.emofree.com)

Today there are many different applications for healing and well-being that employ kinesiology as a tool. The Energy Kinesiology Association has been formed to act as an umbrella organization to represent the field of kinesiology. (See www.EnergyK.org)

## The Energy Impact of Visualization

Now I'd like you to do a simple exercise that will demonstrate how your mind can affect your body. Once you have that experience, we'll be reversing it so you can see how your body affects your mind. Visualization, the simple act of seeing something in your mind's eye, has many applications. It is one of many simple processes that can help you more easily reach the sales goals you want to achieve—and even take them to a new level of success.

Many studies confirm that "seeing" an activity in your mind's eye in as much detail as possible has a profound effect on the body's performance of that activity. Olympic and professional athletes have been trained to visualize every step of their routine or activity, all the way through to receiving the gold medal. One of the first to publicize the role of this body/mind connection in her success was Mary Lou Retton, a U.S. gymnast in the 1984 Olympics. Retton's coach taught her to do a visualization process each time she did her routine. She scored a ten on her last vault and won a gold medal. In total, she won five medals, the most won by any athlete at that Olympics.

Another example of the powerful positive effect of visualization comes from a research study of middle school kids. Three groups of seventh-grade boys and girls were asked to roll a ball at a target. The first group had thirteen hits on the first attempt. This group then practiced rolling the ball at the target for five minutes a day for seven days. When they were re-tested, they averaged a 70 percent improvement at hitting the target. The second group had twelve hits on their first attempt, almost as good as the first group. But then, instead of practicing with the ball, they were instructed to visualize rolling the ball and hitting the target. They practiced this visualization for five minutes a day for seven days. When they were retested using the actual ball, their improvement in hitting the target was 68 percent, almost as good as the group that had practiced with the ball.

The fascinating part of the study came with the third group. They also started out averaging twelve hits. Members of this group spent two-and-a-half minutes doing the visualization technique and then another two-and-a-half minutes actually rolling the ball every day for seven days. When they were retested in rolling the ball, this group had 31 hits, an improvement of 160 percent. The combination of visualization and physical action gave them a huge advantage over the groups that only physically practiced with the ball and the group that only did the visualization.[12]

To experience how powerful and fast visualizing is and how it can impact your body and your mind, do this simple exercise:

## Arm Rotation Exercise

1. Stand up in a place where you can stretch your arms and rotate them without bumping into anything.
2. Keeping your feet firmly rooted in place, raise your right arm up in front of you like you are pointing to an object in the distance.

---

12 Cecelia A. Prediger, "Performance Enhancement Through Visualization," *Research Quarterly for Exercise and Sport,* Fall, 1988.

Begin to rotate your arm slowly to the right until you reach your discomfort point. Hold it there for a second, noting how far your body has turned and where you are pointing towards with your fingers.

3. Rotate back to the front and put your arm down.

4. Now raise your right arm again and rotate to the right for a second time, noting how far your body has turned this time and where you are pointing with your fingers.

5. Rotate back to the front and put your arm down.

6. Close your eyes and, *without any movement of your body,* just visualize that you are raising your arm again and see your arm rotating to the right. This time see your arm rotating in a complete 360-degree circle with absolutely no pain or discomfort. Hold that thought for a few seconds. Then visualize that you are returning your arm back to the front position and then lowering it.

7. Now, with your eyes open, remembering to keep your feet firmly rooted in place, again raise your right arm up in front of you. Begin to rotate your arm slowly to the right until you reach your discomfort point. Hold it there for a second, noting how far your body has turned this time and where you are pointing towards with your fingers.

8. Rotate back to the front and put your arm down.

Were you surprised as to how much farther you could turn this third time? In my seminars, almost everyone is able to rotate farther after doing the visualization versus just doing the physical rotations the first two times. This is to demonstrate to you the power of your mind on your body. This applies to you as a salesperson, enabling you to visualize and focus on the goals, directions, and results you want to achieve. In the next chapter, we will show you how Brain Gym allows you to experience the reverse of the mind affecting the body by seeing your body's power to affect your mind.

# CHAPTER 3

# Choosing Your Preferred Method of Biofeedback Response

In the Brain Gym process you have the option of using one of three different methods of internal biofeedback response. Follow these instructions and you will discover for yourself the amazing ability your body has to simply and easily tell you what it finds positive and beneficial and what it finds negative and difficult in the selling process.

The three Methods of Internal Biofeedback Response are:
1. Muscle Checking with a Partner
2. Self Muscle Checking
3. Noticing

Let's look at them one by one.

## Muscle Checking with a Partner

With this method you'll need to find a partner so you can "muscle check" each other. If you don't have a partner handy, read on anyway—and be sure to do the muscle checking on a partner at a later time.

Muscle Checking with a Partner involves your partner applying physical pressure to your arm muscle. As you'll see, you don't have to be physically strong to do the check or to be checked. The key concept in the checking is that everything around us and within us can affect our muscle strength. Basically, when you apply a steady pressure on your partner's extended arm, her arm will stay up and remain switched-on when she is exposed to a positive thought or a situation that she views positively. Her arm muscle will be switched-off and come down when she is exposed to a negative thought or a situation that she views negatively. This will make more sense to you as you proceed.

In some cases, the results of muscle checking can be influenced by the people involved or by the environment. In order to avoid impacting the results, both the person doing the muscle check and the person being checked should avoid facial expressions, especially smiles and frowns, and there should be no music playing.

There are two ways to do Muscle Checking with a Partner—one method uses a hard pressure and the other uses a lighter pressure. First we'll look at the way to do it using the hard pressure.

### *Muscle Checking with a Partner Using Hard Pressure*
### Step I. Finding Normal Response

Before doing a muscle check for any specific stimuli, you need to check the person in neutral to find their normal response level.

1. Face your partner. Ask if he has any pains or discomforts with either arm or shoulder. If not, continue this process. If your partner has an issue, then use the arm and shoulder that does not have any pain or discomfort. If both are in pain or discomfort, then do not do this process.

2. Ask your partner to raise one arm up from the side of the body so it is at a right angle to the body and level with the shoulder, with the thumb pointing toward the floor. Imagine a bird with a wing outstretched and you'll have the correct arm position. The other arm remains at the side of the body.

3. Now place one of your hands on your partner's extended arm, just above the wrist. Place your other hand on your partner's opposite shoulder.

4. Instruct your partner to resist as you push down, firmly and steadily, with a hard pressure, on the extended arm. As you are about to push down on your partner's arm, say out loud to your partner "Ready—resist." You are not attempting to force her arm down; her arm should stay fairly level while you are applying the pressure. You do want it to be a hard, steady pressure on the arm in order to

measure her normal level of resistance. You should press firmly for several seconds and then release.

If you would like to see a video of Jerry doing muscle checking, you can go to www.Teplitz.com/media/keynote/keynote1.html and watch a 16-minute video demonstration.

If her arm goes down more than an inch or two during this check for her normal response level, you are using too much force. If that occurred, then do it again, remembering that the amount of pressure applied should be based on the person's level of strength. As an example, you would press harder when you are muscle checking a football player and more gently if you are muscle checking a petite person.

When you apply the pressure on the extended arm, you are checking a muscle called the lateral deltoid. As you'll experience in Step II, when a negative stimulus occurs, your partner's arm will go down easily when you apply the same amount of pressure. This will signify through the deltoid muscle that the entire body's energy level is in a switched-off state. When the arm stays up, it will indicate that the person's energy is switched-on. You can use other muscles in your body to do muscle checking, such as the leg muscles; however, the deltoid muscle is easy and conveniently located for this purpose.

**Step II. Muscle Checking a Stimulus**

Now that you've found the person's normal response level, you are ready to do a muscle checking procedure for a specific stimulus. If, during the muscle checking, the person's arm that is being checked becomes tired, you can simply have the person switch to the other arm. Just be sure to check the "new" arm first for its normal level of resistance before you do any further checking.

We'll start out with a muscle checking procedure that shows how your partner's thoughts impact her body's energy by having her think about a negative sales experience she has had.

1.  Check your partner for Normal response as we did in Step I above.

2. While your partner keeps her arm extended, ask her to close her eyes and think of a very negative sales experience. Ask her to nod her head when she has this thought firmly pictured or felt in her mind. Then tell her to resist while you press down. Her arm will go down easily even if she is resisting with all her might. This means thinking this negative thought has switched her off.

3. Now tell your partner to resume the arm-extended position while thinking of a very positive selling experience. Again, ask her to close her eyes and nod her head when she is focused on this image. Then tell her to resist as you push down. Her arm will stay level and it may feel even stronger than when you first checked her for Normal response. She is now demonstrating a switched-on response to the muscle checking.

4. Switch roles and have your partner check you.

You will probably notice that when your partner thinks about a very negative experience, it takes very little pressure to push the arm down. Conversely, when the person thinks about a very positive experience, the arm stays switched-on even if you use more pressure when attempting to push it down.

### *Muscle Checking with a Partner Using Light Pressure*

Now that you know how to muscle check using strong pressure, you can experience this alternative method which uses much less pressure. The same muscle will respond with one-fifth of the pressure used in the "hard pressure" muscle checking. This is helpful because a person's arm tends to tire after a few rounds of hard pressure checking. With the lighter pressure, this fatigue is avoided. Another difference in the Light Pressure Muscle

Checking method is that the person who is being checked is the one who determines when he is ready for the pressure to be applied by saying "push." Because there is a tendency for a person to hold his breath when the person doing the checking presses, possibly affecting the results, the word "push" is stretched out to become "Pussssshhhhhh." This keeps the person breathing. Here's how to do Light Pressure Muscle Checking:

**Light Pressure Muscle Checking for Normal Response**

1. Face your partner.
2. Ask your partner to raise one arm up from the side of the body so it is at a right angle to the body and level with the shoulder, with the thumb pointing toward the floor. This is the same position as in hard muscle checking.
3. Place just two or three fingers of your hand just above his wrist. Put your other hand on his opposite shoulder.
4. Ask your partner being checked to say "Pusssshhhhh" when he is ready to resist and then lightly push down on his arm for couple of seconds, using just a fraction of your strength. He should be able to easily keep his arm up. If you also look at his shoulder, there should have been no movement taking place. If there was, it means you need to press more lightly. In that case repeat this light pressure again so that there is no movement in the shoulder. This will give you the correct "reading" of the amount of pressure to use with Light Pressure Checking.

When you do the Switched-On Selling Balances in the upcoming chapters you will have the option of using either Light or Hard Pressure Muscle Checking. Keep in mind that both of these types of Muscle Checking

*Pusshhh*

require a partner. If you don't have a partner available, you'll need to use a Self Muscle Checking or a Noticing method as your biofeedback response mechanism instead. They are explained in the next section.

There are several things to watch for to make sure the Light Pressure Checking gives you an accurate response. Let's look at the example of the muscle checking we did earlier in this chapter for a negative sales experience. As you'll recall, when the person who was being muscle checked *thought* about a negative sales experience, this thought caused her body to switch off and her arm went down. Though it is rare, let's imagine that you got inappropriate results from this muscle checking— meaning that your partner's arm stayed up when she thought of the negative experience. There are a couple of reasons you might be getting an inappropriate response. They include:

- *Recruiting Other Muscles:* Your partner could be *recruiting* other muscles to help prevent her arm from going down. To do this, she may tilt the whole side of the body up or just raise the shoulder area up. If you observe recruiting, tell her to make sure to have the thumb pointing downward and to only tighten the shoulder muscle as this more specifically isolates the lateral deltoid muscle which is the muscle you are using to measure your response.
- *Faders:* Your partner could be a *fader*. When you press down with this lighter pressure, she may initially appear switched-on with the arm staying up. However, if you continue to hold the pressure for a couple of seconds, her ability to keep her arm up will begin to fade and her arm will go down. Therefore, it's important to press on a person's arm for several seconds so you don't miss the person who is a fader.

*Looking for a Mushy Arm Response:* The arm may only go down a little bit as you are checking your partner while she is thinking the negative thought. That's okay. I describe this as the arm going "mushy." With the lighter pressure you are only looking for subtle differences between the arm staying switched-on and becoming switched-off. (If you are unsure of what "mushy" is, you can do the Hard Muscle Checking described in Chapter 2 as you will get a clearer reading of what is switched-off; however, keep in mind your partner's arm might tire faster. Before doing the hard pressure, warn him that you are switching to using this level of pressure.)

**Light Pressure Muscle Checking for "Yes"/"No" Responses**
Light Pressure Muscle Checking is also used to get "yes" or "no" answers to questions. To determine how this works, follow these instructions:
1. Follow steps 1 through 4 of Light Pressure Muscle Checking for Normal response.
2. Say out loud to your partner who is being muscle checked: "Your body will demonstrate a 'yes' response." Then ask your partner to say "Pusssshhhhh" as you muscle check his arm with the light pressure. His arm will stay up.
3. Say out loud to your partner: "Your body will demonstrate a 'no' response." Then ask your partner to say "Pussshhhhh" as you muscle check his arm; his arm will go down. (Remember to be aware of recruiters and faders as discussed above.)

As amazing as it may seem, through the use of muscle checking your body is capable of answering specific questions. The person being checked or the person doing the checking can ask questions framed in a "yes" or "no" format. This ability to obtain answers to "yes" and "no" questions allows you to access and understand how all parts of the selling process are affecting your selling abilities both consciously and subconsciously.

## Self Muscle Checking Methods

The pioneers in this field, such as Dr. John Thie and Bruce Dew found that it is also possible to get biofeedback responses from the body by muscle checking yourself. Self Muscle Checking is the second method of physical biofeedback response that I use when I am teaching a Switched-On Selling seminar.

There are six different self-muscle checking methods presented here to get "yes/switched-on" or "no/switched-off responses" from your body. Most people find that one or more of these six methods work well for them; although every now and then I encounter a person for whom none of them work. So you'll need to experiment with each of them to see if any work for you and, if several do, decide which one you prefer to use. (If you're one of those for whom none of the Self Muscle Checking methods work, you will need to do Muscle Checking with a Partner or one of the Noticing methods which is presented in the next section.)

### *Self Muscle Checking Method 1: Links in a Chain*

1. Place the tip of your thumb and the tip of your index finger of one hand together as though you are making an "okay" sign or a circle. Hold them together firmly.

2. Link together the index finger and thumb of the other hand inside the circle made by the first hand. It's as if you are forming two links in a chain. You will first be determining a Normal response level by attempting to pull your two circles apart. Use a steady, strong pressure but don't pull so hard that you pull the circles apart. Ask your body (silently or out loud) to give you a "yes/switched-on" response as you attempt to pull your links apart. You should be unable to pull your fingers apart with this level of force.

3. Ask your body (silently or out loud) to demonstrate a "no/switched-off" response and again attempt to pull your links apart. This time, the links should be easily broken and you should be able to pull your fingers through.

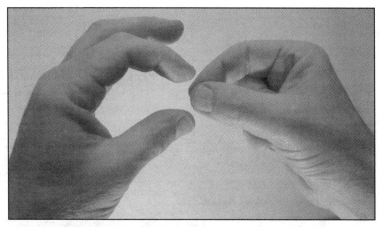

4. If you don't notice a difference, then you'll need to see if the next method works for you.

### *Self Muscle Checking Method 2: Threading the Needle*

1. Once again place the tip of your thumb and the tip of your index finger of one hand together as though you are making an "okay" sign or a circle. Hold them together firmly.

2. With the other hand put the pads of your index finger and thumb together. Now, insert these two fingers into the circle formed by the two fingers in Step 1. It's as if you're threading the eye of a needle with your second hand. Expand these two inner fingers so you are pushing against the fingers in the outer circle. Don't push so hard that the outside circle fingers break contact.

3. Ask your body (silently or out loud) to give you a "yes/switched on" response and attempt to open the two inner fingers. The outside circle fingers should remain in contact.

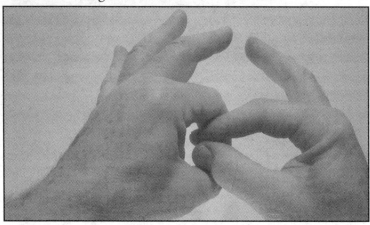

4. Ask your body (silently or out loud) to demonstrate a "no switched-off" response and attempt to open the two inner fingers. This time, the outer circle formed by the thumb and index finger should separate when you push against it with the fingers that are on the inside.

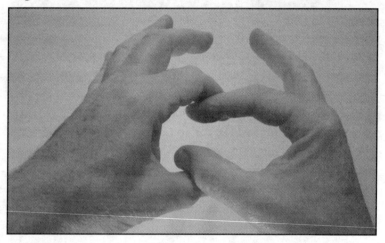

If you don't notice a difference, go to the next method.

### *Self Muscle Checking Method 3: Index and Middle Finger*

Using one hand, place the pad of the middle finger on top of the index finger nail. With the middle finger, push down on the index finger. Say the "yes/switched-on" statement and the index finger will stay straight.

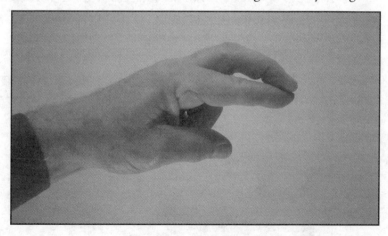

Say the "no/switched-off" statement and the index finger will bend downward. If you don't notice a difference, go to the next method.

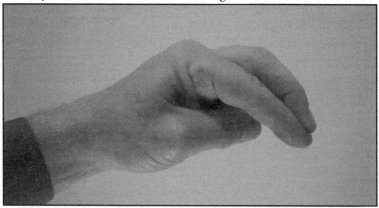

### *Self Muscle Checking Method 4: Thigh Muscle*

While sitting in a chair, raise one foot a few inches off the floor. Place your hand on the thigh muscle. Say the "yes/switched-on" statement and push down on your thigh muscle. It will stay up. Say the "no/switched-off" statement and the leg will go down. If you don't notice a difference, go to the next method.

"Yes/Switched-on response."   "No/Switched-off response."

### *Self Muscle Checking Method 5: Skin Response*

On each hand lightly and quickly rub your index finger and thumb together. While you're doing that, ask your body to demonstrate a "yes/switched-on" response. The fingers should continue to move easily. Next, ask for a "no/switched-off" response while continuing to rub the fingers together. It will become sticky and harder to move the fingers. If you don't notice a difference, go to the next method. (While you can do this with one hand only, I like people to do it initially with both hands in case one hand is more sensitive than the other.)

*Note:* This method of Self Muscle Checking of rubbing the finger and thumb together is based on the same principle as a lie detector test in which the electrical resistance of the skin, called the galvanic skin response, is measured. The galvanic skin response registers immediate changes in the skin's conductivity, which varies when the nervous system triggers changes in the body's internal state.

### *Self Muscle Checking Method 6: Body Rocking*

In this method, the body "rocks" or tilts slightly forward for a "yes/switched-on" response and slightly backward for a "no/switched-off" response.

1.  To get a "yes/switched-on" response:
    Stand with your eyes closed. Say silently to yourself that your body will identify a "yes/switched on" response. You should feel your body tilting forward slightly. This forward tilt will be your "yes/switched-on" response.
2.  To get a "no/ switched-off" response:
    Stand with your eyes closed. Say silently to yourself that your body will identify a "no/switched-off" response. You should experience your body tilting backward slightly. This backward tilt will be identified as a "no/switched-off" response.

Once you have determined this baseline for the body rock, you can use this as your method of self muscle checking. You can also do it with your eyes open.

As I said earlier, one of these Self Muscle Checking methods works for most people. If that's not the case for you, you'll have the option to explore the two alternate ways to do Noticing that is introduced below.

## Noticing

Noticing relies on you to notice what is going on inside your body as your *inner guide*. With Noticing, you'll need to pay special attention to your feelings, posture, body sensations, and breathing. Noticing is an easy method of biofeedback response because it simply involves becoming attuned to your body's constant internal communications system. With this method you stop what you are doing and *notice* the feelings and sensations that may be causing you to be switched-on or switched-off. There are two methods of Noticing. You can use whichever one you are more comfortable with. Let's begin with the first Noticing method.

### *First Noticing Method—Observing Your Body's Responses*
In this first Noticing technique you will observe what's going on in your body. To do this technique you'll need to stand up and put your hands at the sides of your body. Read the instructions below and then follow them without adjusting your body's position. You are just observing your body's responses.

1. Close your eyes and think of a negative sales situation. Really focus on your negative thoughts about it.
2. Keeping your eyes closed and without adjusting your body, observe your physical posture for a few seconds.
3. Next, observe your breathing for a few seconds.
4. Observe if you are you experiencing discomfort or pain in any parts of your body.
5. Finally, observe what's going on in your mind. What kind of thoughts are you having? Is your mind churning?

What did you observe? While there is no one right answer, most people report that they observed that their physical posture was slumped, their breathing was shallow, they had pain somewhere on their body and their mind was churning. I call these responses a switched-off response. If your observations were different, that's okay. Remember, Noticing is not judging, it's just paying attention to what's going on in your body.

Now let's have you do the same thing again except this time you are going to be focusing on a very positive selling situation. Again, you are just observing your body's responses you are not adjusting it.

1. Close your eyes and think of a positive sales situation. Really focus on your positive thoughts about it.
2. Without adjusting your body, first observe your physical posture for a few seconds.
3. Next, observe your breathing for a few seconds.
4. Observe if you are still experiencing discomfort or pain in any parts of your body?
5. Finally, observe what's going on in your mind, in particular, any thoughts that you are having.

So what did you observe? When thinking of a positive sales situation most people report that they observed that their physical posture was upright, their breathing was deeper, they had no pain in their body and that their mind was calmer. I call these responses a switched-on response. If your observations were different, that's okay. Again, Noticing is not judging, it's just paying attention to what's going on in your body and your mind, but it is great feedback that enables us to observe the ways our thoughts immediately affect our mind-body system.

The positive response you had in your body and mind will be used as your definition of a yes/switched-on response as you go through the book. The negative response you had will be used as a no/switched-off response.

### Second Noticing Method—Using Reference Points

To use this method, you will have to first establish specific locations on your body to what it means to have a "switched-on" or "switched-off" response. The visualization technique that follows will help you establish this baseline. You can also apply your responses to getting a "yes" or a "no" response.

*To locate a "switched-on" response in your body:*

Sit quietly with your eyes closed and visualize or remember a past experience that you feel was positive and fulfilling. As you begin to recall this experience in your mind, take a few seconds to intensify the thought. Once this feeling is intensified, locate it at a specific place on your body. Take ten to fifteen seconds to intensify the feelings at this location on your body. Say silently to yourself that this location will be identified as a "switched-on" response. Some examples of these internal feelings and awareness can include:

- A feeling of ease or automatic movement
- A feeling of joy
- A physical sensation somewhere in or on your body
- A subtle movement
- A smile coming across your face
- A specific movement of eye, head, etc.
- A feeling of calm

*To locate a "switched-off" response in your body:*

Continue sitting quietly with your eyes closed and visualize or remember a past experience that was difficult or negative. As you begin to recall this experience in your mind, take a few seconds to intensify the thought. Once this feeling is intensified, locate it at a place on your body. Take ten to fifteen seconds to intensify the feeling at that location on your body. Say silently to yourself that this location will be identified as a "switched-off" response. Some examples of these internal feelings and awareness can include:

- A feeling of doubt
- A feeling of disappointment
- A physical sensation somewhere in your body
- A frown coming across your face
- A specific movement of your eye, head, etc.
- A feeling of tension
- Uncertainty in a new situation

Once you have determined this baseline for the internal experience of "switched-on" reactions and the comparable "switched-off" reactions of the body, you can use this as your method of Noticing.

### Using Noticing in the Balance Process

You can use either of the Noticing techniques as you go through the balance process at the end of each of Tony's upcoming chapters. Just notice if your body is feeling the way it did when you were thinking the positive thought in the first Noticing method. If you are using the second Noticing method then you will get a response on a place on your body where you identified either the "yes/switched-on" response or the "no/switched-off" one.

## Which Internal Biofeedback Response Method Should You Use?

As you are going through the balance steps in the coming sections of this book, you will choose which method you will be using: Muscle Checking with a Partner, Self Muscle Checking or Noticing. Even if you are doing one of the physical checking methods, I suggest that you also start Noticing internally whether you are switched-on or switched-off so you are also becoming comfortable with that method.

You can also switch methods each time you do a Balance. I find that each individual will gravitate to one or two methods that they are most comfortable with. Just start out with one of them and go from there.

## The Energy Impact of Your Thoughts and Attitudes

All of the biofeedback response methods will glean the same results. They prove that negative thoughts and experiences, such as rejection on a sales call is draining to your body's energy. And simply thinking about a positive sales experience is strengthening. However, while your energy is raised by thinking of a positive thought, *it is switched-on only as long as you maintain that thought.* If you return to viewing the situation negatively again, the draining impact will return. The following exercise will demonstrate this.

The instructions below use Muscle Checking with a Partner, although you can use Self Muscle Checking or Noticing if you prefer. Just adapt the instructions as needed.

1. Check your partner for Normal response.

2. Ask your partner to close her eyes and visualize a negative sales experience in her mind. Muscle check her with either the Hard or Light Pressure method. Her arm will go down, meaning she's switched-off.

3. Next, ask her to switch the negative experience and find something about it to view positively even if it's just being glad the situation is over.

4. Ask her to shake her head to indicate that she has made the switch.

5. Tell her to resist and press down on her arm. Her arm will remain switched-on.

6. Have her repeat the negative thought again and check her. Her arm will go down again.

7. Have her repeat switching to the positive thought again and check her. Her arm will remain switched-on this time.

This exercise shows us once again the incredible power of the mind. By *changing your mind* about how you view a situation, you can temporarily alter the impact the experience is having on you. All you need to do is to *decide* to think positively about the experience. While this is easy to say, I grant you that it can be difficult to maintain positive thoughts about a situation that is challenging to you. That's why I say it is temporary. And that's where the Brain Gym Balances, which you'll learn in Chapter 6, come into play. These Balances are life changing because they re-educate your mind-body system to eliminate your negative thoughts about the stressful aspects of the selling process. For example, in the Balance for Positive Selling, you'll learn two Brain Gym techniques that in only two minutes will allow you to completely eliminate the negative charge from the negative sales situation you just pictured. This means after you've completed that Balance, you'll be able to think of the same situation but it will no longer have a negative impact on you.

# CHAPTER 4

# BRAIN GYM MOVEMENTS AND EXERCISES

There are four main components to a Brain Gym Balance:
1. Biofeedback responses from the body using one of three methods you just learned in Chapter 3: Muscle Checking with a Partner, Self Muscle Checking or Noticing
2. Brain Gym movements and exercises, which are covered in this chapter.
3. Calibration (which you'll learn in the next chapter)
4. The Balance itself, which you'll learn in Chapter 6.

## Using Brain Gym Movements to Re-Wire and Rebalance the Brain

Brain Gym movements are specific exercises that correlate to the way in which we perform different tasks, motor skills, and activities. In his book, *Brain Gym and Me,* Paul Dennison, the creator of Brain Gym, explains it this way: "The Brain Gym movements have been designed to activate various cognitive functions, including communication, organization, and comprehension. The movements are effective because they activate the brain in specific ways that ready us for learning. Brain Gym strengthens the physical skills involved in the learning process, and when we feel physically prepared to meet the day, the mental aspect of our learning comes more easily."[13]

When used in conjunction with Balances (which you'll learn in the next chapter), these movements re-wire and rebalance the neural pathways in your brain. As I previously discussed, when you have an

---

13  Dennison, Paul D., Ph.D., *Brain Gym and Me*, Edu-Kinesthetics, Inc., 2006, page 46.

aspect of the sales process you don't like to do, it's harder for you to do that part of the process, if you can do it at all. In minutes, the Brain Gym movements balance and integrate your brain's hemispheres quickly and easily so what was difficult becomes easy. Some of the Brain Gym exercises require physical movement, which you should do slowly, while others are easy positions which you simply hold for thirty to sixty seconds.

These Brain Gym movements and exercises are very easy to do and, as research both my clients and I have conducted have repeatedly shown can have an extremely favorable impact on your selling abilities, especially when you plug Tony's selling strategies into your sales efforts. (Tony's strategies begin in Chapter 6 and then are continued in Part II.)

## The History of Brain Gym Movements

Many of the Brain Gym movements in this book were originally developed more than seventy years ago in the fields of behavioral optometry and sensorimotor training, while others were adapted from acupressure and yoga. Over the years, a number of leading pioneers in the learning and health fields created their own variations on these movements.

In the early 1970s, Dr. John Thie created Touch for Health, a system for natural health that included brain integration techniques as well as other methods such as acupressure, touch, and massage to improve postural balance and reduce physical and mental pain and tension. Dr. Thie's book, *Touch for Health* was published in 1973.

In addition to the work of Dr. Paul Dennison and Gail Dennison, who created Brain Gym, a number of other pioneers have used or adapted Brain Gym movements in their work. They include: Gordon Stokes and Daniel Whiteside *(One Brain: Dyslexic Learning Correction and Brain Integration)*, Dr. Carla Hannaford *(Smart Moves: Why Learning is Not All in Your Head)*, Dr. Charles Krebs *(A Revolutionary Way of Thinking)*, Sharon Promislow *(Making the Brain/Body Connection)*, Laurie Glazener *(Sensorcises: Active Enrichment for the Out-of-Step Learner)* and Cecilia Koester *(Movement Based Learning for Children of All Abilities)*. Educators and trainers who use Brain Gym movements in their classes include Paul Scheele of Learning Strategies Corporation and T. Harv Eker of Peak Potential Training.

## Brain Gym Movements and Exercises

I'd like you to do the Brain Gym movements and exercises in this section so you will understand how simple and easy they are to do. As you continue with this book, you will be told which Brain Gym movements to use as you do each of the Balances. It is the Brain Gym movements and exercises that actually re-wire and rebalance the brain.

In addition to learning how to do each of the Brain Gym movements below, you will also find an explanation of what that specific movement does in the brain and the body. It's important that you do Brain Gym movements slowly to allow the brain and body to make more neural connections.

### Alphabet 8s

Center a piece of paper in front of you. With a pen or pencil, begin by drawing continuous and overlapping infinity symbols.

Figure 1

Step 1: Draw three infinity symbols using your left hand, then three using your right hand, then three using both hands together. Your eyes remain focused on the point of your pen or pencil.

Step 2: *The letter a:* Draw three infinity symbols with your normal writing hand. Without stopping, draw a lower case letter "a" on top of the left-hand side of the 8. Without stopping, do two more infinity symbols.

Figure 2

Step 3: *The letter b:* Draw three more infinity symbols. Without stopping, draw a lower case letter "b" on the right-hand side of the infinity symbol. Again without stopping, do two more infinity symbols.

Step 4: *The letter c & d:* Repeat the same sequence, drawing a letter "c" on the left side of the infinity symbol, and then repeat the same sequence drawing a "d" on the left side.

You only need to draw these four letters.

Figure 3     **59**

*Explanation:* Alphabet 8s integrates the left and right visual fields while also increasing left and right hemispheric integration. This may enhance creative writing, spelling, and peripheral vision. Reading, writing, and concentration skills improve.

## Arm Activation

Lift your right arm straight up toward the ceiling, keeping it as close to your ear as you can. Place your left hand on the front of the right arm muscle. As you slowly and gently exhale through your mouth, do an isometric movement by pushing your right arm against your left hand without letting your right arm move. Continue pressing for about seven seconds. Inhale as you relax your pressure. Place your left hand on the back of your arm and press again for seven seconds. Repeat this procedure, pressing against the outside of your right arm and then against the inside of your right arm.

Repeat the entire sequence for the other arm.

*Explanation:* The Arm Activation lengthens the muscles of the upper chest and shoulders, where muscular control for both gross and fine motor activities originates. This movement improves focus and concentration, enhances one's ability to express ideas, and helps one have a longer attention span for doing paperwork.

## Balance Buttons

Place three or more fingertips about two inches behind your left ear, about three finger widths away from the ear. Place your other hand on your belly button. Rotate your eyes slowly from the far left side to the far right side and back again. Continue to rotate the eyes back and forth without straining. Hold for thirty seconds.

Change hands and repeat on the other side.

*Explanation:* Balance Buttons appears to stimulate the body's balance system through the inner ear. This restores your sense of equilibrium, relaxing your eyes and the rest of your body and freeing your attention for easier thought and action. This improves one's ability to make decisions, concentrate and problem solve.

## Belly Breathing

Place your hands on your stomach. Begin by inhaling through the mouth into the stomach. Your hands should move outward with the inhalation. Begin to exhale through your mouth, in short little puffs of air as if you are keeping a feather floating in the air. Continue to exhale until your lungs feel empty. Again inhale deeply, filling your stomach. This time don't exhale in short puffs; instead do a slow and complete exhalation.

Repeat this deep inhalation and exhalation for three or four breaths.

*Explanation:* Belly Breathing improves oxygen consumption and blood circulation to the brain and the central nervous system while increasing one's energy level. It improves diaphragmatic breathing which has been found to improve both reading and speaking abilities.

## Brain Buttons

Place one hand on your belly button. With the thumb and fingers of the other hand, locate the two hollow areas below the collarbone. The hollows are one or two inches away from the sternum which is the bone that runs down the center of the chest.

Rub these areas vigorously for thirty seconds.

*Explanation:* Brain Buttons improves digital and hand-eye coordination for writing and computer work while relaxing neck and shoulder muscles. It also improves body balance and enhances energy levels.

## Double Doodle

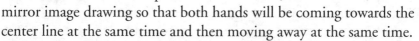

Take a piece of paper. You are going
to draw mirror images on the paper
using both hands simultaneously.
Begin by drawing a line down the
center of the paper. Next, draw identical
doodles on each side. Keep in mind this is
mirror image drawing so that both hands will be coming towards the
center line at the same time and then moving away at the same time.

Continue for thirty seconds.

*Explanation:* Double Doodle is drawing with both hands, which
establishes directionality and orientation in space relative the center
line running down the front of the body. This assists in developing
hand-eye coordination for improved writing skills, spelling, and math.
It also improves ones ability to skim and scan what is being read.

## Earth Buttons

Place two fingers from one hand under the lower lip.
Put the heel of the other hand on the navel with the
fingers pointing downward. Wherever your fingers
reach, rest them on the body. With just your eyes
moving and not your head, look at the floor for
a couple of second and gradually raise your eyes
to the ceiling as if you are tracing your eyes up a
straight column and then immediately look down
again. Keep moving your eyes from down to up.

Repeat this ten times. Continue to breathe.

*Explanation:* Earth Buttons are located on the
center line running down the front of the body.
Holding these points stimulates the brain and relieves
mental fatigue, as well as increases organizational skills
and enhances the ability to focus on close objects such
as computer screens.

## Hook-Ups

This movement is done in two parts:

**Part I ...**

Sit in a chair or stand and clasp your hands together. Whichever thumb is on top will be considered your primary side. Release your hands and extend your hands in front of you with the back of each hand facing the other. Cross the primary side hand over the top of the other hand and intertwine your fingers. Draw your hands under and into your chest. Cross your primary side ankle in front of the other ankle. Place your tongue against the roof of your mouth, one quarter inch behind your front teeth. The first time you do this keep your eyes closed. Keep breathing through your nose. Hold for thirty seconds to one minute.

**Part II ...**

Uncross your legs and release your hands. Place the fingertips of both of your hands together forming a teepee. Keep your eyes closed the first time you do this, the tongue up, and continue to breathe. Hold for thirty seconds.

*Explanation:* Hook-ups is a variation of an exercise originally developed by Wayne Cook, an expert on electromagnetic energy. Part I connects all the energy circuits in the body at the same time and stimulates the movement of any blocked energy. Touching fingertips in Part II balances and connects the two hemispheres of the brain. This reduces stress while raising comfort levels in new situations, enhances balance and coordination, and improves one's ability to listen and speak.

## Lazy 8s

Place your left arm extended straight out in front of you with the thumb pointing towards the ceiling. Focus your eyes on that thumb. Without taking your eyes off of it and keeping your head facing straight forward, trace the infinity number 8 in the air slowly and smoothly.

Begin to trace your Lazy 8 at the center point of the 8 and go up and to the left side with your hand. Do three full Lazy 8s with one hand, then do three with the other, and, finally, do three of them with both hands clasped together. Remember to keep your head facing forward.

*Explanation:* Lazy 8s integrate the left and right visual fields while also increasing left and right hemispheric integration which improves balance and coordination. Many people report better binocular vision and increased peripheral vision after doing the Lazy 8s. Reading, writing, and comprehension skills improve as these tasks become easier.

## Space Buttons

Place two fingers above the lip. Place your other hand on your tailbone. While keeping your nose facing straight ahead, look up with your eyes toward the ceiling for a few seconds. Imagine a column in front of you and gradually lower your eyes down the column to the floor. Immediately raise them to the ceiling and hold them for a couple of seconds in that position. Repeat the movement ten times up and down while you continue to breathe.

*Explanation:* Space Buttons are located at the top and bottom of the central nervous system which includes: the spinal column, back brain, midbrain (which is the portion of the brain located behind the eyes and nose) and cerebral cortex. Holding the two points stimulates movement throughout the system, which improves attention, focus, motivation, and intuition for decision-making.

## The Calf Pump

This movement is similar to a runner's stretch.

Place your hands shoulder-width apart against a wall, leaning your body at a 45-degree angle to the wall. Place your right foot in front of the body with the knee bent and extend the left leg out straight behind you.

Imagine you have a string coming out the top of your head. As you exhale, raise your left heel off the floor, while keeping your left leg straight. As you inhale, lower the left heel to the floor.

Do this a total of three times then switch leg positions and repeat three times. The more you bend the knee in the front, the more stretch you will feel in the back of the calf.

*Explanation:* The Calf Pump restores a more natural length to the muscles and tendons in the back of the body. This improves attention and focus while creating a deeper feeling of relaxation. It also improves written and spoken communications while increasing the ability to plan, complete projects, and anticipate closing.

## The Cross Crawl

March in place like a drum majorette. As your right arm swings up, your left leg moves up, allowing you to touch the right hand to the left knee (or as close as you can get). Next, swing the left arm and the right leg up so that you touch the left hand to the right knee. When you make this movement, you are automatically crossing the midline of your body. (The midline runs down the center of the body. If you draw a straight line from your nose down past the belly button, that's where the midline is located). Continue to do The Cross Crawl movement slowly.

Continue for thirty to sixty seconds.

### *Variations of The Cross Crawl:*

There are other ways to achieve the effect of The Cross Crawl. You might want to experience each of them.

- Instead of touching your hand to the opposite leg, reach your hand down and touch the opposite heel. Continue by alternating touching opposite hand to the opposite heel.
- Use your elbows instead of your hand to touch the knee. Continue by alternating touching the opposite elbow to the opposite knee. This variation of The Cross Crawl stretches the core stomach muscles and gives the body even more stretch.
- Move your left heel behind you and touch your heel with your right hand. Continue by alternating touching opposite hands and heels behind the body.

*Explanation:* When you use one hand to touch the knee on the opposite side of your body, you are crossing the midline of your body. This activates both sides of your body simultaneously. It is called a heterolateral movement because both the left and right hemispheres of the brain have to cooperate for your left hand and your right knee to be at the correct place at the same time so that contact can occur. Because The Cross Crawl activates both brain hemispheres simultaneously, it engages the brain for coordinating visual, auditory, and kinesthetic abilities. This exercise improves such skills as listening, reading, writing and memory-all valuable tools for selling.

## The Elephant

Stand with your feet about shoulder-width apart. Bend your knees point your right arm straight down to the floor in front of you. Lean your head so that the right ear touches or is close to your right shoulder. Point your finger and begin to trace an infinity figure 8 in the air with your extended arm. Focus your eyes slightly past your hand. Keep breathing as you move. Start by going up the center and to your left side. As you do the upper loop of the 8, straighten your legs. As you do the lower loop, bend your legs again.

Do this a total of three times, then repeat with the left arm.

*Explanation:* The Elephant releases muscle tension in the neck, often caused by a chronic avoidance of turning the head to listen, which may have inhibited our ability to perceive sound. The Elephant restores natural flexibility to the neck. It also integrates the left and right sides of the brain for increased ability to listen and comprehend, short and long term-memory.

## The Footflex

While you are sitting in a chair, rest your left ankle on top of your right knee. Form a V with your left hand and place it on both sides of the back of the calf muscle right below the back of the knee. Place the right hand on both sides of the Achilles tendon about an inch or two above the anklebone. At both locations where you are grasping the muscle, begin to pull your fingers apart. This will give a slight stretch to the back of the calf muscle. Continue this pulling while you point and flex the left foot up and down for thirty seconds. Don't move your foot side to side or in a circle. Just move it up and down.

Repeat with the right ankle on the left knee.

*Explanation:* The Footflex restores the natural length of the tendons in the calf area. It relaxes the reflex desire to hold back which increases our abilities to communicate, concentrate, lead, and complete tasks.

## The Grounder

The Grounder is similar to a fencing lunge movement. Stand with your legs a comfortable distance apart—as though you are going to do a split. Point your right foot toward the right. Point your left foot straight ahead of you. Now bend your right knee as you exhale, keeping the left knee straight. Keep your hips facing squarely forward. Protect the right knee by bending no further than the middle of the right foot.

Repeat three times and then repeat it in the other direction, keeping the right knee straight and bending the left knee.

*Explanation:* The Grounder lengthens and relaxes the hips, which stabilizes the balance of the body. This increases comprehension, short-term memory, self-expression, and organizational skills including doing phone and desk work.

### The Owl

Take your left hand and with the thumb and fingers grasp the right shoulder muscle near the neck that runs along the top of the shoulder. Squeeze the muscle firmly and lift it slightly with your left hand. Inhale and turn your head to look back over your right shoulder. Now as you exhale, rotate your head to the left side, to look back over the left shoulder. Do this rotation a total of three times and then drop your chin to your chest while you relax your shoulder muscle.

Repeat using the right hand on the left shoulder.

*Explanation:* The Owl releases tension in the shoulder and neck muscles. This restores range of motion for turning the head and increases the circulation of blood and energy, which improves listening comprehension as well as thinking, speaking abilities and the use of a computer.

## The Positive Points

Just above the center of both eyebrows and halfway up to the hairline, you will find a slight bump where the head curves. Place three fingers together lightly on the bumps. Close your eyes and breathe.

Hold the points for thirty seconds to one minute.

*Explanation:* The Positive Points are acupressure points for diffusing the fight-or-flight reflex, which releases emotional stress related to specific memories. Holding these points will also release temporary memory blocks and increase your ability to hear other points of view. It will allow you to give presentation in a more relaxed manner.

## The Thinking Cap

Using both hands simultaneously, start at the top of each ear by placing the index and middle fingers together behind the curved part of the ear. With the thumb at the front of the ear, begin to "unroll" the curved part of the edge of the ear by pulling the thumb back and flattening the curved part of the ear. Continue all the way to the bottom of the ear.

Repeat this a total of three times.

*Explanation:* The Thinking Cap helps the brain tune out distracting sounds and noises and tune into meaningful rhythms and sounds. This movement increases listening ability, short-term memory, and abstract thinking skills.

# CHAPTER 5

# CALIBRATION

There is one more process to learn before we put it all together and do a complete Brain Gym Balance. Calibration is helpful for two reasons: 1) on its own, Calibration prepares your body and mind for learning new information, and 2) when done before Muscle Checking with a Partner, Self Muscle Checking or Noticing, Calibration aligns your body-mind system to achieve more accurate results.

I call this procedure Calibration because it correlates to calibration in a scientific setting. When two pieces of scientific equipment are used in the same experiment, they are first adjusted or calibrated to each other so the readings are consistent. This assures that both pieces of equipment are measuring the same levels. If researchers don't calibrate the equipment before they begin the experiment, they have no way of knowing if their results are accurate. This relates to the Brain Gym work because—just like the pieces of equipment in the scientific experiment—it is possible for the body-mind to be out of sync in a way that will cause inaccurate responses. For example, if you are doing Muscle Checking with a Partner and either the person being checked or the person doing the checking is not in calibration to the other, the person being checked may give inaccurate responses.

Let's say you are doing the process of Muscle Checking with a Partner with a partner named Susan. If you muscle check her on the statement, "My name is Susan," and she muscle checks "no," you obviously have an inappropriate response. That means that something in her system *or* in your system is causing an imbalance that led to this inappropriate response. This can be prevented if both of you do the calibration procedure before you do the muscle checking. Calibration can also be used while you are in the middle of a Balance session. Let's say the person being balanced starts to have inappropriate responses, such as being switched-off to something that clearly should be switched-on. Just stop the Balance and do another round of Calibration and then proceed with the Balance.

If you are using Self Muscle Checking or Noticing for your biofeedback response method, and therefore don't have a partner to calibrate with, the process of Calibration is still helpful because it will prepare you internally so your mind-body is ready and able to learn.

Calibration allows us to confidently rely on the results of the biofeedback response method we are using. There are two ways to do Calibration. There is a fast, easy way, which is presented below. This faster method is also found in the instructions for each of the Balances in this book. And, for those who want more details, there is a more comprehensive calibration process, which also explains the underlying validation behind each of the steps. This more extensive version of Calibration is presented in Appendix A on page 231. If you prefer, you can substitute the version in Appendix A whenever you are asked to do the Calibration procedure.

In the Calibration procedure below I'll explain the purpose of each of the parts. Then, beginning on page 76, you will find the condensed procedure for doing each step in Calibration.

**Part 1:  Need for Water**

Water is the most important liquid you can put into your body. About 60 to 70 percent of your body is water and it is the one liquid you must absolutely have, in one form or another, to live. Of course, many of us already know about the necessity of drinking eight glasses of water a day. But what many of us do not know is exactly why we need so much water.

Your body must be sufficiently hydrated so it can send the chemical and electrical signals needed in order to perform both mentally and physically. If you are dehydrated, these signals will be interfered with which will interfere with a myriad of bodily functions, including:

- As a major component of blood, water is part of the delivery system that carries oxygen to the brain and each cell in the body.
- The digestive system uses several gallons of water daily to process food.
- Water is crucial for the lymphatic system, which is responsible for carrying away waste products.
- Because it ionizes cell salts in the body, water has a major role in producing the electrolytes that are necessary for the electrical activity to occur across the membranes of your cells.
- Every joint in your body requires water as a lubricant so that your movements will be smooth and painless.
- Your brain, which is about three-quarters water, requires sufficient hydration to perform all of the chemical reactions that are required to run the body.

The feeling of thirst in your mouth is slightly ahead of the body's Need for Water. By the time you begin to feel thirsty, you are moving into in a state of dehydration. Even a small loss of water will have serious consequences, including a laboratory-proven measurable decrease in physical performance. This negative impact occurs when you lose a mere two percent of your total body water, which is equivalent to the average amount lost at the end of an hour of exercise. If your water loss amounts to somewhere between six and seven percent, you will experience definite symptoms of dehydration and weakness. If you rely solely on thirst to remind you to replenish water when you exercise, it may take your body a full 24 hours after a workout to return to proper hydration levels.

Even as you sit and read this page, your body is maintaining a constant, light perspiration. The amount of perspiration increases as you experience stress or undergo more strenuous activities. You also lose water in the form of vapor every time you exhale. Both air conditioning and heat cause additional dehydration of your body. On a typical day, you excrete two and one-half quarts of water from your body. And if you exercise for an hour or more or live in a dry climate, you could lose up to an additional quart.

When exercising, even a mild degree of dehydration can affect your performance. Here are some guidelines to make sure that doesn't happen:[14]

- Drink 8 ounces of water before exercising.
- Drink approximately 4 ounces of water every 15 minutes or so while exercising.
- Drink eight ounces of water twenty to thirty minutes after you finish exercising.

Herbal teas and watered-down fruit juices and sports drinks can be counted toward your water intake. But beverages that contain caffeine, such as coffee, tea, and some sodas, have a diuretic effect and actually remove fluid from the body. This means for every cup of caffeinated beverage you drink, only two-thirds of it can be counted towards your water intake for the day.

Simply sipping water throughout the day is a way for you to maintain your mental fitness. It may also help reduce the amount of fatigue you feel on days when you've drunk a lot of caffeinated drinks.

To complete this part of Calibration, drink some water.

**Part 2: Electrical Circuitry**

To get in Calibration for electrical circuitry, which is designed to make sure electrical signals are flowing through the body, do the Brain Buttons in Chapter 4 on page 61.

**Part 3: Activating**

In this part of Calibration, you are switching your system into gear for doing the physical Brain Gym movements. You are activating your body to move. To do this, do The Cross Crawl in Chapter 4 on page 65.

**Part 4: Stress Reduction**

The Stress Reduction aspect of Calibration is designed to dial

---

14 Guidelines for water needs during exercise from a study by Evian Water.

down your adrenal glands if they are over-stimulated. If the adrenal glands are secreting adrenalin, then your body is in a "fight-or-flight" modality, which is a survival state. In this mode, it changes the circuitry and the operation of the entire body and you are not able to learn new information or fully experience new situations. To make sure the stress response is not activated, simply do the Brain Gym movement called Hook-ups in Chapter 4 on page 63.

**Part 5: Method to Use**

If you are working without a partner and using a Noticing or Self Muscle Checking method as your biofeedback response, just determine the Noticing (page 51) or Self Muscle Checking (page 45) method you will be using.

*If you are working with a partner,* do the Muscle Checking for Normal response with a hard or light pressure, which you learned in Chapter 3 (see page 39). *If you are working with a partner,* it's important to do this step so you get the feel for your partner's level of resistance. It's also the opportunity for the person who is being muscle checked to give you feedback, especially if the pressure is too hard for his arm.

**Part 6: "Yes"/"No" Response**

Do Muscle Checking with a Partner, Self Muscle Checking or Noticing for "yes" or "no" responses on both of the following statements:

- "My body will demonstrate for me a 'Yes' response." (With Light or Heavy Pressure Checking your arm should stay up.)
- "My body will demonstrate for me a 'No' response." (With Light or Heavy Pressure Checking your arm should go down.)

When you have completed the Calibration process you should get appropriate responses to both of these statements—switched-on for the "yes" and switched-off for the "no."

Now that you understand the concept, here are the step-by-step instructions for doing Calibration in a Balance.

## Calibration Procedure

1. **Need for Water:** To make sure you are not dehydrated simply drink some water.
2. **Electrical Circuitry:** To make sure your electrical circuitry is operating efficiently, do Brain Buttons (page 61).
3. **Activating:** To make sure your body is ready to move, do The Cross Crawl (page 65).
4. **Stress Reduction:** To make sure your stress response is deactivated, do Hook-ups (page 63).
5. **Biofeedback Method to Use:** Select whether you will do Muscle-Checking with a Partner, Self Muscle Checking, or Noticing (page 54).
6. **"Yes/No" Response:** Use the biofeedback response method you chose to ask the body for a "yes" and then a "no" response in Chapter 3 (page 45).

**NOTE:** When you are in the middle of a Balance, you may begin to get inaccurate or questionable results. While this rarely occurs, it is possible and, in case it does, I want you to know what to do about it. Simply repeat the Calibration procedure, and then proceed with the Balance, beginning at the same point where you started to get the inaccurate results.

# CHAPTER 6

# THE BRAIN GYM BALANCES

Now we're ready to put all the pieces together and learn how to do a Brain Gym Balance.[15] It is the Balance that will actually re-educate the brain, allowing you to discover the specific aspects of the selling process that are difficult and then *eliminate the internal blockage to that goal.* After doing the Balance, your brain will no longer perceive the blockage to that part of selling and, without effort, you will achieve greater selling success.

Paul Dennison, who developed Brain Gym, explains a Balance like this: "Balancing, a term to which we in Educational Kinesiology gave a new meaning, refers to the entire Brain Gym process, including having a specific goal for each session; performing the action you're intending to improve (or some activity symbolic of same); experiencing the joy of movement; and noticing what works for you."[16]

As I mentioned earlier, you can think of a Brain Gym Balance as re-wiring and rebalancing the circuitry of your brain from a *fear / survival focus,* which is triggered by past negative or stressful experiences, to a *present time / choice focus.* Through this re-wiring process, you will create new neural pathways that will make it easier to achieve the success you are looking for in your sales career.

You may recall the discussion on the part of the brain called the amygdala in Chapter 1 (see page 21). In most cases, the goals that you find difficult to achieve are triggering an automatic stress response in the amygdala. This response causes your amygdala to send a signal to the body's fight-or-flight survival mechanism, which keeps you in the

---

15   The Brain Gym Balances used in Switched-On Selling are a variation of Brain Gym Balances as taught by Brain Gym International.

16   Dennison, page 45.

old "it's difficult to achieve" or "I can't do that" mental programming of that aspect of the selling process. You are caught up in the memory of negative experiences and stuck in your inability to achieve your goal. The Balance reprograms the brain so the signal will be directed to the cerebrum instead, allowing you to choose a new response related to that situation. By doing the Balances, you will be switching off the amygdala's stress response while you will be *switching on* the cerebrum's ability to choose new responses for the different aspects of the selling process.

For example, if a salesperson who is challenged by doing cold calling does a Balance for being able to easily and effortlessly make cold calls, the amygdala will no longer bring up the old programming that made cold calling difficult. The Balance creates new wiring in the amygdala, allowing the cerebrum to now take over and respond with new, positive programming. After doing the Balance, she will find cold calling much easier and less stressful. In fact, she may even find it enjoyable—even when she's still got a challenging sales quota to meet and is under pressure to perform.

So now let's look at what happens in a Brain Gym Balance:

1.  First, after you've read through each of Tony's chapters, write down the parts of the selling process that he's just covered that you have difficulty with or find stressful. These are what I call Trigger Points or Hot Button issues. They show up as a small inner voice or feeling that says, "I can't do what Tony says I need to do in this aspect of the sales process." For example, your Trigger Point or Hot Button issue might be, "When I walk into the prospect's office, my palms start to sweat and I get nervous." After you write the Trigger Point down, write a positive statement in the column next to it. In writing this positive statement allow yourself to see you solving or successfully doing whatever it was that triggered you. Using the example above, you might write "I am calm and confident when I walk into a new prospect's office."

2.  In the next part of the Balance, you will find a list of pre-selected positive statements that relate to other aspects of the

selling process that may be different from the material in that chapter. You'll use Muscle Checking with a Partner, Self Muscle Checking, or Noticing to determine if you are switched-on or off for each statement.

3. You'll now have an opportunity to write your own statement if you feel that there is an aspect to the selling process missing from the statements in number 2.

4. Next, you'll do a physical role play or action for twenty seconds or so to represent each of the statements that are switching you off. While I know some people feel awkward doing this "role play," it is important to do because it activates areas of the brain that are involved with those aspects of the selling process. Doing the role play will determine whether you are switched off when you physically make believe you are doing the activity.

5. The fourth step will be for you to determine if you will include past events that relate to the current situation in this Balance.

6. The fifth step will be for you to do all Brain Gym movements and exercises listed in that chapter, which will integrate your entire system for the goal.

7. The sixth set will be for you to go through *all* the statements again—both your Trigger Point positive statements and the other statements to confirm that you are switched-on for all of them.

8. Next, you'll repeat the physical role play or action *only for the actions you had been switched-off for the first time through the Balance.*

9. Finally, if you have a partner, you will celebrate your success. If you were doing Self Muscle Checking or Noticing, give yourself a big pat on the shoulder.

**NOTE:** Each Balance is presented with step-by-step instructions, so you don't have to remember the steps now.

As you go through the chapters, it is possible that you will find that you are switched-on for all of the statements in one or more chapters. In other words, no Trigger Points or Hot Button issues came up for you as you read through that chapter and you are not switched-off for any of the additional statements because you don't have any difficulties or issues with that particular part of the selling process. If you find that's the case, you will go directly to the Brain Gym exercises and movements in that section. By doing the Brain Gyms even though you were already switched-on for the topics that were covered in that chapter, you will further strengthen your abilities related to that specific area of selling. Those who are already good will easily move from being good to being great and even more successful.

## The Steps to a Brain Gym Balance

Now you are ready to do your first complete Balance, the Balance for Positive Selling. Then, in Part II (Chapters 7 through 13), you'll find Tony's sales strategies for the following additional aspects of the selling process, coupled with Balances specifically designed for each of those topics:
- Goal setting
- Enjoying selling
- Pre-approach planning
- Prospecting
- Presentation
- Follow-up
- Prosperity

## Positive Selling Through Collaborative Selling

Let's begin this part of the process with Tony sharing with you Positive Selling Through Collaborative Selling.

**Identifying Your Trigger Points:**

As you read through Tony's strategies in this chapter, be aware of any Trigger Points or Hot Button issues that surface in your mind. For example, in Tony's upcoming section, at one point he discusses making contact with prospects in person. For some people, reading that might bring up an immediate discomfort or negative thought. It's those feelings and thoughts that we're re-wiring and rebalancing with the Brain Gym Balance. For the purpose of this particular exercise, think of and focus on one negative past sales situation. That's what you'll focus on during the Balance. (As I shared earlier, in Part II of this book, we'll go into all the other aspects of the sales process and you'll be instructed to write down the Trigger Points and Hot Button issues that arise as you're reading Tony's strategies.)

The world of business has changed and continues to change dramatically and rapidly. Markets have grown from local to national to global. Technology no longer offers a competitive advantage, and customers have become much savvier. All of these changes and more have created an environment in which salespeople must adopt new attitudes, learn new skills, and gain a new understanding of how to approach their markets and work with customers.

No doubt, you have seen this quantum shift and its consequences in your industry: your competitors have increased in number and become more aggressive. Your products or services are more difficult to sell than in the past. It has become a challenge just to differentiate your company from your competitors, and price issues are a constant problem.

The upshot of these market influences is that the differentiated products of yesterday are the commodities of today. Instead of making differentiation easier, technology has made differentiation more difficult. Differentiation is, however, the *only* way to be successful in today's market. Differentiation must come from quality, price, or service; and few companies can survive competing on price. This is a monumental challenge that every company faces. It is a challenge met by collaborative selling, a system in which salespeople can create differentiation and its accompanying competitive advantage every time they go after business.

Collaborative selling begins with a commitment to the long-term. Today's customers buy differently, so today's salespeople must sell differently. Customers know there is no urgency to buy because good deals, good salespeople, and good companies come along every day. Price is less of an issue because buyers are not just interested in great deals; they want great relationships. Today's customers are looking for *measurable* quality in the products and services they buy.

The transition to collaborative selling and the emphasis on long-term relationships is evident in the words and phrases that are used to describe modern buyer-seller relationships: strategic alliances, sustaining resources, single sources, integrity, values, and ethics.

Today's customers are looking for long-term relationships with companies who will be reliable resources over the long haul. Collaborating companies are networking their computer systems to expedite order-entry, just-in-time inventory control, and electronic payment. Strategic alliance, partnering, collaboration call it what you want is taking place throughout the world on a macro level (industry to industry) and on a micro (salesperson to customer) level.

Collaborative selling means handling every aspect of the sales process with a high degree of professionalism. There are six basic steps that describe how the collaborative sales process unfolds:

**Target**

The first step is a marketing necessity: understand exactly what the product/service is and identify the specific markets that can best use it. This is done on a company level in their marketing plan and should be done by individual salespeople as well. It takes some time, but careful planning focuses effort and provides a greater return on time and money invested. Collaborative salespeople know they must concentrate on prospects who have a high probability of buying.

## Contact

The first step after targeting a market is to contact them in a cost-effective and professional way. Naturally, this would be some combination of email, letter, phone call and personal contact. The right combination of contacting strategies ensures that collaborative salespeople create high-perceived value before they call on their prospects.

When contact is made, collaborative salespeople set the stage for a cooperative, working relationship. They convey their desire to explore needs and opportunities. They build credibility and trust. They express their sincere desire to be of service, and they make their competitive advantages known without jumping into a presentation.

## Explore

In this stage of the collaborative sales process, salespeople convey the message: "Let's explore your business situation to see if there are needs to fulfill or opportunities on which to capitalize."

During the explore stage, collaborative salespeople conduct research, meet with their prospects frequently, and do whatever it takes to become an expert on their prospect's business. The give-and-take relationship that develops sets the stage for in-depth exploration of options that may culminate in a sale. Collaborative salespeople make it clear that they want to help, not just make a sale. If, after information-gathering, collaborative salespeople find that their products are not appropriate for their prospects, which is unlikely due to their careful target marketing, they will forego the sale, but have made a friend and business contact. The Explore stage of selling, and in fact the entire Collaborative Selling philosophy, is built around the following phrase— *"Prescription Before Diagnosis is Malpractice."*

## Collaborate

It is at this point after an in-depth exploration of a prospect's situation that collaborative salespeople talk about their products or services. Naturally, they are discussed in the context of prospects' needs or opportunities.

Collaborative salespeople never dictate solutions to their prospects. Instead, they form "partnerships" in which prospects play an active role in the search for the best solution. The collaboration phase of the sale is conducted in the spirit of "let's work together on the solution and together build a commitment to its successful implementation." This team-approach to problem solving ensures that prospects will be committed to solutions. By making customers equal partners in problem solving, collaborative selling reduces or eliminates the risk that is inherent in the customer's decision-making process.

## Confirm

Keep in mind that, in every phase of the collaborative selling process, the salesperson and prospect have communicated well. Collaborative salespeople move on to the next phase of the sales process only after they have received assurances that their customers are in agreement with them on everything that has been discussed.

This agree-as-you-go process eliminates the need to "close" the sale as most objections have surfaced long before this point. If resistance does occur, the salesperson simply gathers more information or clarifies a detail.

With collaborative selling, the sale is a matter of *when* and not *if.* Confirming the sale is the logical conclusion to an on-going communication and problem-solving process. There is no need to "close" them. People commit when all their buying criteria are met!

## Assure

This phase of the collaborative sales process begins immediately after the sale has been confirmed. Collaborative salespeople keep in touch after the sale. They communicate regularly about delivery dates, installation, training, and other relevant matters. They make sure their customers are satisfied with their purchases. They help customers track their results and analyze the effectiveness of the solution.

Collaborative selling is the key to differentiation on the micro level. It represents an obsession with quality and customer satisfaction. It reflects a high degree of professionalism and a primary focus on relationships rather than transactions. It is clear that collaborative selling is a mutual-win situation; one that provides increased security to both parties. This increased security is exactly what customers want and need, given the market changes that are occurring so rapidly.

Collaborative selling is a philosophy and practice that is being used today by enlightened salespeople; and it is clearly the sales process of the future. Collaborative selling helps professional salespeople build large, loyal customer bases that generate future sales, provide referrals, and act as lifetime annuities.

---

# BALANCE FOR POSITIVE SELLING

You are now ready to learn how to do a Balance.

In Step 1 of the Balance for Positive Selling you will pick a negative sales situation to focus on. It may be from what was triggered in the information you read in Tony's section above. Did a negative thought come up? For this Balance you can also pick a negative sales situation you've experienced. It could be having been rejected on your first call of the day, or any situation from your past that is still in your memory. This past situation can be continuing to negatively influence your selling effectiveness.

What this Balance will do is literally remove the negative charge attached to that experience from your brain in two minutes. You'll still have access to the memory of this situation but it will no longer have a negative impact when you bring it to mind. Sounds miraculous, doesn't it? The fact is that when you think of the negative experience, it will be like you are reading about it in a novel. You will no longer carry the "negative charge," so thinking about it will no longer be a stress.

## STEP 1. TRIGGER POINT:

> Pick a negative sales situation that was triggered by reading Tony's strategies or, if nothing he shared in this section triggered you, pick a negative sales situation that recently happened to you or a situation from your past that still bothers you.

**STEP 2. CALIBRATION: Preparing for the Process**
If necessary, refer to the more detailed instructions on Calibration on page 71.
1. **Need for Water:** To make sure you are not dehydrated simply drink some water.
2. **Electrical Circuitry:** To make sure your electrical circuitry is operating efficiently, do Brain Buttons (page 61).
3. **Activating:** To make sure your body is ready to move, do The Cross Crawl (page 65).
4. **Stress Reduction:** To make sure your stress response is deactivated, do Hook-ups (page 63).
5. **Method to Use:** Select whether you will do Muscle-Checking with a Partner, Self Muscle Checking or Noticing (page 54).
6. **"Yes/No" Response:** Use the biofeedback response method you chose in Chapter 3 to ask the body for a "yes" and then a "no" response (page 45).

**NOTE:** When you are in the middle of a Balance, it's possible you may begin to get inaccurate or questionable results. While this rarely occurs, it is a possibility. In case it does occur, simply repeat the Calibration procedure, then continue with the Balance, beginning at the point where you began to experience the inaccurate or questionable results.
Let's now have you experience the next steps to the process.

**STEP 3. CHECKING THE ISSUE: Visualization**
In this step, picture in your mind the situation you selected in Step 1. Focus on the negative about it. Once you have it fully visualized in your mind, do Muscle-Checking with a Partner, Self Muscle Checking or Noticing.
Are you Switched-On or Switched-Off?
In almost all cases, because you picked a negative or stressful situation, you will be switched-off and your arm will come down. If this is did not occur, then pick another negative or stressful situation to use for this Balance so that your response is switched-off. Next, proceed to Step 4.

## STEP 4. CHOOSING TO INCLUDE THE PAST

In a moment you will be saying out loud yourself (or to your partner, if you are working with a partner):

"My system now incorporates, in the most appropriate way, all relevant past events, known and unknown, into the Step 3 experience."

*Let me explain the purpose of the Step 4 statement before you do Muscle-Checking with a Partner, Self Muscle Checking or Noticing. In effect, you are asking your mind-body if there are any negative events that happened earlier in your life that relate to the current situation you visualized in Step 3.*

*Here's an example. Perhaps someone yelled at you yesterday on the telephone and you froze in fear. The triggering event that caused you to freeze might have occurred when you were six years old when someone yelled at you on the telephone and you froze. This memory is still stored in the part of the brain called the amygdala. (See page 21.) The amygdala will receive the electrical signal from the ear that you were yelled into. As part of its job, the amygdala is looking for a memory of when you were yelled at before and/or felt threatened when you have been on the telephone. Assuming the amygdala finds a time when you were six years old, it then sends a signal to trigger the adrenal glands to secrete adrenalin, which puts the body in the fight, flight or in this case freeze response.*

*The statement you're reading out loud is asking your amygdala if there is something from the past stored there. If your system finds something, you are asking if it wants to get rid of that past trigger (or triggers if there is more than one situation) during the current Balance.*

*In effect a "yes" response means, "I do have triggers from the past on this subject in the amygdala and my body does want to discharge them during this Balance."*

If you are Noticing, just observe if it feels as if there is something from the past involved with the current situation. If it feels like there is, you can simply choose to incorporate it into the current Balance. If you are Self Muscle Checking or using Muscle Checking with a Partner, then a "Yes" response means your amygdala has some triggers from the past on this subject stored in it and your body will include them in the current Balance even if you don't know exactly what the situation or situations are in your conscious mind.

If you get a "No" response, it is not wrong. It simply means either there is nothing in your past related to this current situation or that the situation is not something that your system wants to deal with at the present time.

Now do Muscle-Checking with a Partner, Self Muscle Checking or Noticing and you'll get either a "yes" or "no" response on this statement: "My system now incorporates, in the most appropriate way, all relevant past events, known and unknown, into the Step 3 experience."

Whether you get a "yes" or a "no," continue on to Step 5.

**STEP 5: TAKING ACTION: Doing the Brain Gym Movements**

Now's the time for you to do the Brain Gym Movements listed below to create the rewiring impact on your body and your mind which will get rid of the negative charge attached to your thoughts. This means the Trigger Point or the negative thought you selected in Step 3 will no longer be operating and controlling your thoughts and actions! (See the instructions and illustrations for each of the Brain Gym Movements in Chapter 4, beginning on page 57.)

- Do Hook-ups (see page 63).
- Do The Positive Points (see page 69).

It should take approximately 2 minutes to do these two Brain Gym movements.

**STEP 6. CHECKING THE CHANGES: Visualization**

Picture the same situation as you did in Step 3 above. When

you have the visual of the situation focused, do Muscle-Checking with a Partner, Self Muscle Checking or Noticing.

You should now be switched-on. The negative charge attached to that situation is gone. You can now think about the situation and not have a negative response.

## STEP 7. WHERE ARE YOU NOW?

Now that you have switched off the negative charge attached to that sales situation and are switched-on, Notice: 1) what you observed happening while you were doing Hook-ups and The Positive Points and 2) how you feel when you think about the situation now. If you have a partner, share your observations with him. (*Hint:* You might have noticed that it became difficult to focus on the negative situation or that your mind wandered off when you attempted to think about it. If so, that's because the negative is no longer being activated.)

## STEP 8. IT'S TIME TO CELEBRATE

If you're working with a partner, congratulate your partner on the successful completion of the Balance for Positive Selling. If you're Noticing or Self Muscle Checking, congratulate yourself.

## Will This Last?

You have now removed the charge from this negative, stressful situation. You might now be thinking, "How long will this last?" Well, the negative stressful energy attached to this situation may be gone forever. If the trigger you focused on was related to what you read in Tony's material, you will now be able to do what he was talking about without being triggered.

However, if something re-triggers you, simply do Hook-ups and The Positive Points while thinking of the negative situation again to get rid of the charge. You can use this Balance for any negative, stressful sales situation that occurs. If your first sales call in the morning is negative, do this Balance to immediately get rid of the charge so you can still create a positive selling day for yourself.

## You're Ready to Proceed

This is the basic format you will be following for all of the other Balances in this book. You are now ready to incorporate Brain Gym into all aspects of the selling process. As I mentioned before, the rest of the book has been divided into eight categories—goal setting, enjoying selling, pre-approach planning, prospecting, presentation, follow-up and prosperity.

---

# THE SWITCHED-ON SELLING QUESTIONNAIRE

Before we go further, we'd like you to fill out the Switched-On Selling Questionnaire. This will allow you to identify your current strong points in the selling process as well as your areas of difficulty. At the end of each Balance in the upcoming chapters, you'll have the opportunity to re-check what has changed for you. Please be honest when you are filling out the questionnaire so you will see clearly what has changed from doing the Balance process.

Place a check mark in the column that most clearly reflects your level of agreement or disagreement with each statement below:

| | | Strongly Agree | Agree | Doesn't Apply | Disagree | Strongly Disagree |
|---|---|---|---|---|---|---|
| 1. | I easily set sales goals for myself. | | | | | |
| 2. | I enjoy selling. | | | | | |
| 3. | I am effective as a salesperson. | | | | | |

| | | Strongly Agree | Agree | Doesn't Apply | Disagree | Strongly Disagree |
|---|---|---|---|---|---|---|
| 4. | I view myself as a successful salesperson. | | | | | |
| 5. | I research potential clients prior to making contact. | | | | | |
| 6. | I easily and comfortably surf the web. | | | | | |
| 7. | It is easy for me to make cold calls using the telephone. | | | | | |
| 8. | It is easy for me to make cold calls in person. | | | | | |
| 9. | I am comfortable in taking on the telephone. | | | | | |
| 10. | I am comfortable with face-to-face visits. | | | | | |
| 11. | I effectively begin the presentation. | | | | | |
| 12. | I develop a rapport quickly with a client. | | | | | |
| 13. | I effectively answer objections. | | | | | |
| 14. | I effectively answer questions. | | | | | |
| 15. | I am comfortable asking for the order and closing the sale. | | | | | |
| 16. | I handle rejection well. | | | | | |
| 17. | I offer my clients other opportunities. | | | | | |
| 18. | It is easy for me to ask my clients for referrals. | | | | | |
| 19. | It is easy for me to write proposals. | | | | | |
| 20. | I provide effective customer service. | | | | | |
| 21. | I easily and effectively complete all paperwork. | | | | | |
| 22. | I view myself as prosperous. | | | | | |

# PART II

## SALES STRATEGIES

BY TONY ALESSANDRA, PH.D.

### *followed by*
## BRAIN GYM BALANCES

BY JERRY V. TEPLITZ, J.D., PH.D.

# INTRODUCTION TO PART II

In this part of the book, Dr. Tony Alessandra shares sales perspectives and strategies that he has taught to many of the most successful salespeople in the United States and many other countries. These sales strategies will help you break through to new dimensions in your career.

After each of Tony's sections, Jerry presents a Switched-On Selling Balance which is specifically designed for that specific part of the sales process. As you read Tony's material, take note of the Trigger Points or Hot Button issues that surface in your mind.

When you find something that feels like a problem or challenge for you in Tony's material, go to the end of the chapter and write down your Trigger Points in the space provided. Next to each Trigger Point, you'll rewrite it as a positive statement, as if you were able to accomplish it easily and effortlessly. Here's the example discussed earlier of a Trigger Point relating to prospecting and the Positive Goal Statement you might write next to it:

| TRIGGER POINTS | POSITIVE GOAL STATEMENTS |
|---|---|
| Example: "When I walk into the prospect's office, my palms start to sweat and I get nervous." | Example: "I am calm and confident when I walk into a new prospect's office." |

Additionally, you will also be given a list of statements that relate to other aspects of the selling process. For each of these statements, you will determine if you are switched-on or switched-off. For example, in the goal setting chapter, some of the other aspects include:
- "I set realistic goals."
- "It's easy and natural to write my goals down."
- "I periodically re-evaluate my sales goals."

Since this book is interactive, you can also add your own goal statements to those that are listed in the aspect section. These goal statements relate to your own personal Trigger Points or Hot Button issues. Let me give you an example that I've heard from salespeople. It goes something like this: You're pulling into a parking space to make a cold call on an potentially important new prospect, and you notice that your mind keeps running through your opening statement. As you get out of your car and start to walk toward the door, you feel your palms getting sweaty. When you get to the reception desk, you find yourself a bit tongue-tied and stumble over some of your words. When the prospect comes out to greet you, you drop the brochure you're carrying. Finally, you're seated in front of him or her, your mind goes blank, and you hear a voice inside you say, "I've blown it now."

If any of this has happened to you, or if you've had other experiences when you've been prospecting that made you feel uncomfortable, gave you a knot in your stomach, a constriction in your throat, or a dry mouth, then you're noticing clues that your energy and abilities are switched-off. If you've heard a little voice inside you say "I can't do that" or "That's going to be too difficult for me to do" then you're noticing an internal doubt that has switched you off. These are all examples of your personal Trigger Points or Hot Button issues.

You are now ready to cover the rest of the program. Enjoy the journey!

# CHAPTER 7

# GOAL SETTING

**Identifying Your Trigger Points:**

As you read through Tony's strategies in this chapter, you may want to write down any Trigger Points or Hot Button issues on page 107 as you go along. Or, if you prefer, you can read the entire chapter and then write your responses. Either way works just fine. (If necessary, review the instructions on Trigger Points on page 95.)

Salespeople are trained to set goals, but find it challenging to balance their personal and their work lives. It is important to realize and accept the fact that many needs must be fulfilled if we are to be well adjusted and happy. Our basic needs fall into seven categories:

1. **Mental:** The functions of your mind—memory, concentration, learning, creativity, reasoning, mathematical ability, etc.
2. **Physical:** The many functions of your body—overall fitness, percent of body fat, skills and abilities, agility, endurance, etc.
3. **Family:** Your relationships with the special people you consider part of your family.
4. **Social:** Your relationships with others outside the family and outside your business.
5. **Spiritual:** Your relationship between you and your Creator; also defined as the philosophical and humanitarian areas of your life.
6. **Career:** Your involvement in your chosen field, both on and off the job.

7. **Financial:** The management of your financial resources and obligations.

In many ways we are like the fragile ecosystem of the environment in which we live. The different elements of our lives are interdependent. One need affects the others, especially when it is grossly neglected. For example, we all know that financial problems affect personal outlook, health, social life, and family life. It is for this reason that practitioners of holistic medicine examine all facets of a person's life when they search for the cause of a physical illness.

There is no escaping the fact that we are complex beings with complex needs. Our needs are dynamic rather than static—that is, they change. At one point in our lives, the development of a career may require more time than our spiritual or family needs. At some other time, physical needs may be emphasized more than social or financial needs. Just because one need is more urgent than others does not mean that the others disappear. They, too, must receive at least a minimal amount of attention. Rarely can a need be completely neglected without unpleasant consequences.

To have a successful career, you need to work at bringing your life into balance. This requires goal setting—identifying the results you would like to achieve for each facet of your life. Only then can you plan the concrete steps and intermediate goals that stand between your present situation and your ideal concept of yourself.

## THE IMPORTANCE OF GOALS

*"Most people aim at nothing in life ...*
*and hit it with amazing accuracy." (Anonymous)*

Such a statement is a sad commentary about people, but it is true. It is the striving for and the attainment of goals that makes life meaningful. Goals, when earnestly pursued, give people reasons to do some things and to avoid other things. Goals give us purpose and channel our energies. It is easy to spot a person who has a clear set of goals. That person is the one who exudes a sense of purpose and determination.

He or she has abundant energy and is willing to put more time and effort into any given task. Being goal oriented helps one become more positive, optimistic, and assertive.

We can think of ourselves as bodies of water. Someone without goals is like a stagnant lake, spread out, with no movement. The lake just sits there motionless at the bottom of a mountain. A goal-oriented person is like a river forging its way through obstacles in its way, the mountains. The river has movement. It is exciting and, in its flow of enthusiasm, it carries with it whatever the current is able to pick up along the way.

In recent years, many studies have focused on productivity. One finding repeatedly confirmed is that people who continuously set, pursue, and monitor their career goals are more productive than people who just "work at a job." Pride in and ownership of one's choices are important ingredients in career satisfaction and success. In contrast, the uninspired worker goes home at the end of the day, having gained nothing more than a few dollars and a lot of aggravation.

Even on the factory-worker level, it has been shown that productivity will increase if a better incentive (goal) is provided for the worker. We all know that pieceworkers are more productive than salaried employees. This proves the "WIIFM" principle: What's In It For Me? The greater the rewards are, the higher the drive is to attain the goals set. The individual chooses the goals with the most desirable payoff.

Almost every speaker, writer, and educator in the area of personal success agrees that committing your goals to paper is a necessary step in committing one's life to attaining those goals. If you take the time to do this, you will stack the odds in your favor and be on your way to becoming more successful than those who do not commit their goals to writing.

The dividends reaped by investing in yourself are unlike any found in the financial world. When you clarify your values and set goals in all the major areas of your life, the right roads appear in front of you like mirages in the desert. Yet, rather than mirages, they are real! Choices become infinitely easier to make, and you have taken a giant step toward living a balanced life.

## Brainstorming

A valuable way of exploring your goals is through brainstorming. In brainstorming, you give free flight to your ideas on a specific problem to be solved. Opening your mind in this way can be valuable. By just letting ideas flow without judging them, you will generate many times the ideas produced through the normal reasoning process. After the abundant ideas have been generated, you can go back to evaluate their usefulness.

Brainstorming unleashes all the creative capacities in our minds. It does this by removing the restrictions and guidelines under which we have been taught to operate. The "rules" for brainstorming are as follows:

- **Suspend all judgment.** This is a time to remove your internal censor. Nothing is unimportant or too silly to include when brainstorming.
- **Think quantity, not quality.** The more ideas you generate, the better the chances are of hitting upon something new and useful. Bad ideas can always be thrown out later.
- **Extrapolate and cross-fertilize.** No matter how nonsensical it may seem, take your ideas to the nth degree. Combine ideas in unusual ways to stimulate new ideas.
- **The wilder, the better.** This is a time to be "way out." Some of the best ideas are unconventional ones.
- **Evaluate later.** Do not close your mind to any suggestions. Let the ideas percolate. An idea that seemed ridiculous yesterday may be ingenious tomorrow.

To brainstorm, find a time when you will not be distracted. Sit comfortably with a pencil and paper. The purpose of the brainstorming session should be stated in the form of a question or a problem to be dealt with. The question must be specific, such as, "How can I increase my inventory of prospective buyers?" Once the question has been posed, you should immediately begin jotting down ideas. It is important to record the first thing that comes to your mind. Do not judge, write! Make notes in brief phrases to save time. After a pre-determined time limit, you can fill in the details of your notes.

After you have finished, review your notes. Examine all the possibilities as they come up. Discard unusable ideas only at the end. It is important and worth repeating that you should suspend all judgment during this exercise. Often wild and crazy ideas, when put together or altered slightly, turn out to be novel, effective solutions. So let yourself go. This is a time to have fun with a creative challenge. You will find that you have a broader range of choices after brainstorming than you thought possible before.

Now that you see how the process works, we would like you to do it. When considering your life's goals, apply the brainstorming process to your goals in each of life's key areas—mental, physical, family, social, spiritual, career, and financial. If necessary, review the list on page 100 so you're clear about each area. Brainstorm each category using the rules we have just discussed. When doing such an exercise, allow approximately two minutes per category, using one page per category. Again, shoot for quantity and let your imagination take over.

Once you have finished, review what you have written and add anything you might have forgotten. When you are satisfied with your responses, look them over and circle the one idea under each category that stands out as being most important. Do not worry about what others might think or what is socially acceptable. Such an exercise allows you to see your goals in black and white, on paper, where they should be.

After completing your review, you should have seven circled semi-finalists from the seven groups. Whether or not there is repetition is unimportant. Examine the seven goals, disregarding which group they came from, and choose the three that are the most pressing to you. Write those three on a separate sheet of paper with the title, "My Three Most Important Goals."

The three goals listed on your separate sheet of paper represent the most important goals in your life at this time. Naturally, your circumstances change from day to day and from year to year. Rarely will a goal endure for your entire life. Whether your goals are short-term or long-range, you can see that such an exercise causes you to identify those things most important to you at this moment.

With all the insight you have at hand, create a hierarchy of goals from the lists compiled. As valuable as it is to isolate your most precious goals, it is equally important to set out some less substantial goals for which to strive. So take the seven categories and list all the secondary goals that you feel are worthy of action. You now have a better idea of where you are and where you would like to be in every facet of your life.

As an example, here is a list that someone might compile:

- **Career Goals:** Make three more sales per week; earn an MBA degree.
- **Family Goals:** Call Mom and Dad once a week; spend ten minutes more each day with my spouse and each child.
- **Spiritual Goals:** Go to church once every week; be more helpful to people every day.
- **Social Goals:** Go to weekly Rotary Club meetings; socialize with more business people and exchange ideas.
- **Mental Goals:** Stop worrying so much about money and success; improve my memory of names; increase my vocabulary proficiency; broaden my general knowledge.
- **Physical Goals:** Eat less junk food; do stress reduction exercises every night; floss my teeth every night; maintain an ideal weight.
- **Financial Goals:** Own my own home; purchase a sports car; provide for an ample retirement fund by the time I am 55 years old.

## Goal Setting Rules

When you have uncovered some goals, it is important to put them in a workable form. Certain rules need to be observed in order to make them effective. Goals must be:

- **Personal**
- **Specific**
- **Positive**
- **Attainable and Challenging**
- **Written**
- **Realistic**

When most people are asked, "What are your goals in life?" they respond with something like, "To be happy, healthy, and have plenty of money." On the surface, this may seem fine, but as goals that lead to actions, they are not sufficient. For goals to be effective and workable, they must meet the following rules:

1. **A goal must be personal.**

   This means that your goal must be something you want to do rather than something that you think you should do. Know your reasons for having the goal. Whether you want to achieve something for status, money, or good health is secondary as long as you want it badly enough to work hard for it.

2. **Your goal must be positive.**

   It is an automatic response to think of the thing you are told not to think about. This is because the mind cannot not think of something when told to do so. We tend to focus on ideas and actions from a positive framework. When you think a negative thought such as, "I will not smoke today," your mind perceives it as "I will smoke today." You end up thinking more about smoking than if you had phrased it differently. "I will breathe only clean air today," is a statement that serves the same purpose and is more effective.

3. **Your goal must be written.**

   Written goals take a jump in status from nebulous thoughts to bona fide entities on paper. Seeing them written out serves as a visual reminder and thus continually reconfirms their importance. They gain credibility just from being written. We have been trained from childhood to give credibility to written statements. This can be seen in the statement from the movie, *The Ten Commandments:* "So let it be written, so let it be done." When things are "put in writing," they become official in our minds. A written goal strengthens our commitment to accomplish it.

4. **Your goal must be specific.**

   If you set your goal by saying, "I will increase my income next year," the chances are that you will not do it. You must be specific in order to avoid the lack of commitment that comes with being vague. A more workable and motivating goal would be, "I will increase my income next year by 10 to 15 percent." This revised statement has several advantages. It defines the increase for which you are striving as well as the range of the desired increase. Giving yourself some leeway is more realistic than expecting to hit your goal exactly on the mark. If you increase your income 13 percent instead of 15 percent, you have still succeeded.

5. **Your goal must be attainable and a challenge.**

   A goal must motivate you to work harder than you have in the past. It must move you forward. Set your goals beyond your reach so that you will have to stretch a bit. The more you stretch, the more limber your goal-achieving abilities will become.

6. **Your goal must be realistic.**

   Everything is relative to time and space. What is unrealistic today may be totally within reason five years from now. For years it was believed that the fastest a man could run a mile was in four minutes. It was unrealistic to aspire to running any faster until Dr. Roger Banister broke the four-minute mile in 1954. Since then hundreds of runners have done the same. In any field, we never really know what the upper limits are. How, then, do we define realistic?

For our purposes, the best definition must come from you and your values. You must ask yourself, "What price am I willing to pay to accomplish this goal?" You should always weigh the payoffs and the sacrifices involved before coming to a conclusion. What's realistic? That's ultimately your decision.

Now that you know the rules for setting goals, you can apply them to the goals you set for yourself. It would be a good idea to make some worksheets and use them for every primary and secondary goal you want to achieve. For each goal, do the following:

1. **Define your goal.**

   Your first task is to determine whether your goal meets all the requirements of the rules listed above. If it does, then write it as clearly as possible at the top of your worksheet.

2. **Examine obstacles that stand in your way.**

   This is a time to guard against negative assumptions and other self-defeating thoughts. Remember the definition of realistic. An obstacle blocks you only if you let it. You should also write down your innovative ways of overcoming obstacles.

3. **W.I.I.F.M.—What's in it for me?**

   Write down why you want to achieve the goal. What kind of payoff is motivating you?

4. **Plan your action.**

   You need to carefully list the steps you will take which will bring you closer to your goal. The smaller the increments, the easier they will be to accomplish. A German proverb says, "He who begins too much accomplishes little."

5. **Project a target date for your goal.**

   State your deadline in a range, such as, "between March 15th and April 1st." Think carefully about the amount of time you need. Too little time will increase the pressure and frustrate you. Too much time may reduce your drive.

6. **Know how you will measure your success.**

   Goals should be described in terms of the outcome of an activity rather than as the activity itself. This is part of being specific. Instead of saying, "I will be running more in four to six months," you could say, "I'll be running three miles instead of two miles in four to six months."

When using your worksheets:
- Fill them out completely and keep them visible!
- Put them in a place where you will see them every day.
- Check off items as you complete them.
- Use them to chart your progress and take pride in your accomplishments.

# BALANCE FOR GOAL SETTING

Brain Gym Balances can be used for any issue or area in your life. However, since this is a sales book, we're going to focus on your sales goals in the Brain Gym Balances. Simply look at the life goals that Tony has shared in this chapter and then look at the Trigger Points and Hot Button issues that came up for you and use this template to do Balances.

The Balance for Goal Setting is designed to reorganize the energy in your brain and body so you can set your sales goals, you are receptive to doing this, and you are switched-on for it. After doing this Balance, a person who didn't previously set goals might still not set them; however, he will now have the capability of doing so if he chooses to. This ability to choose will have been anchored into the brain and body.

## STEP 1. TRIGGER POINTS:

We're now going to give you the opportunity to identify the Trigger Points that came up for you in this chapter and write them down. Does anything that you've just read act as a "Trigger Point" or a "Hot Button issue" for you?

On the left side of the column below, briefly write the aspect(s) of Tony's information that is triggering you and switching you off. On the right side, write a goal statement about that Trigger Point in a positive statement, as if you have already easily and effortlessly accomplished it. Even though the Trigger Point may have some negative feelings or thoughts attached to it, or the situation currently feels like a problem or challenge, it's important to write the goal statement with positive language because this is the direction you want to create in the new wiring in your brain. This is what the Brain Gym movements will assist you in switching on.

If more than one Trigger Point comes up, write all of them down in the left column. If there's not enough room below, use another piece of paper. After you have written all your Trigger Points, again write a positive goal statement for each Trigger Point.

If you didn't have any Trigger Points come up for you in this section, that simply means that you're comfortable with setting goals in your sales career; however, as you continue to do this Balance, you may find that other triggers come up for you and you'll have the opportunity to do the Balance on them. If this is your situation, then skip to Step 2 in the Balance below.

| TRIGGER POINTS | POSITIVE GOAL STATEMENTS |
|---|---|
|  |  |
|  |  |
|  |  |
|  |  |
|  |  |

**STEP 2. CALIBRATION: Preparing for the Process**

If necessary, refer to the more detailed instructions on Calibration on page 71.

1. **Need for Water:** To make sure you are not dehydrated, drink some water.

2. **Electrical Circuitry:** To make sure your electrical circuitry is operating efficiently, do The Brain Buttons (page 61).
3. **Activating:** To make sure your body is ready to move, do The Cross Crawl (page 65).
4. **Stress Reduction:** To make sure your stress response is deactivated, do Hook-ups (page 63).
5. **Method to Use:** Select whether you will do Muscle Checking with a Partner, Self Muscle Checking, or Noticing (page 54).
6. **"Yes"/"No" Response:** Use the biofeedback response method you chose in Chapter 3 to ask your body for a "yes" and then a "no" response (page 45).

**NOTE:** When you are in the middle of a Balance, it's possible you may begin to get inaccurate or questionable results. While this rarely occurs, it is a possibility. In case it does occur, simply repeat the Calibration procedure, and then proceed with the Balance, beginning at the point where you began to experience the inaccurate or questionable results.

**STEP 3. CHECKING THE ISSUES: Statements and Actions**
    **A. TRIGGER POINTS:**

If you wrote down any statements from Tony's material, do Muscle Checking with a Partner, Self Muscle Check, or Noticing on both the negative goal side and the positive goal side of what you wrote. If you are Muscle Checking with a Partner, read the statements out loud. You should be switched-off for the statements in both columns. If you are not switched-off, then what you thought was a negative Trigger Point is not one.

    **B. ASPECTS OF GOAL SETTING:**

Make the following statements one at a time and do Muscle Checking with a Partner, Self Muscle Checking, or Noticing to determine if your body is switched-on or off after saying each statement. If you are Muscle Checking with a Partner, read it out loud. Place a check mark next to any statements for which you are switched-off.

_____ 1. "I set personal goals."

_____ 2. "I set specific goals."

_____ 3. "I set positive goals."

_____ 4. "I set attainable and challenging goals."

_____ 5. "I set realistic goals."

_____ 6. "It's easy and natural to write my goals down."

_____ 7. "I periodically re-evaluate my sales goals."

_____ 8. "I keep accurate records on the selling process."

_____ 9. "I complete my goals in a timely manner."

**C. YOUR ISSUES AND CHALLENGES:**

Write your own positive affirmations if there are still aspects of goal setting that you still feel are an issue or challenge for you. While you have written those as positive statements, you should be switched-off when you do Muscle Checking with a Partner, Self Muscle Checking, or Noticing because your brain is not yet switched-on for achieving it. It is also okay not have to have any statements to add.

_____ 10. _____

_____ 11. _____

_____ 12. _____

If you were switched-on for all of these statements, that means you don't have any major issues with this aspect of the selling process. If this is the case, skip to Step 5 and do the Brain Gym movements and exercises to move yourself to an even higher level of success.

**D. ACTIONS:**

Now do a physical action, role play, or visualization for each of the Trigger Points you wrote down or the statements you placed a check mark next to in Step 3-B or C for which you were switched-off. Do each action for twenty seconds or so and then do Muscle Checking with a Partner, Self Muscle Checking, or Noticing as soon as you complete each action. Place a check mark next to each action for which you are switched-off.

**Purpose of Doing Actions:** *Let me explain the purpose of this step. You should do actions only for the Goal Setting statements above that caused you to be switched-off. This part of the Balance allows you to check your response to the physical impact of attempting to do the various elements of the goal-setting process. In this part, you will be discovering if you are switched-off at the level of the body.*

*It's actually possible to be switched-off for a statement in Step 3-A, but be switched-on when you do the action in Step 3-B. This means your block for this part of goal setting is not in the physical doing of the action; rather, your block is solely in your mind. For example, after you read the statement, "I set specific goals," you might be switched-off when you do Muscle Checking with a Partner, Self Muscle Checking, or Noticing, and when you do an action related to "I set specific goals," you might be switched-on.*

*After you do the Brain Gym movements and exercises in this Balance, the final outcome will be that you will be switched-on for all of the statements, as well as any actions for which you had been switched-off.*

_____ 1-6. If you were switched-off for any of the statements numbered 1 to 6 in step 3-B above, actually write a sales goal in the space below that includes the issues you were switched-off for: i.e. positive, specific, positive, attainable and challenging and/or realistic. For example, if you were switched-off for the statement, "I set specific goals," write a goal that you view as specific. As an example, writing that you want to make a lot of money in the next year is not specific. Instead, writing a goal such as "I will make $100,000 in the next year" is specific.

Several items can be included in one goal statement. For example, specific and measurable can be combined into this statement: "I will make $102,000 next year in twelve $8,500 increments."

Write your own goal below:

_____

_____

_____

_____

_____

Now that you've written your own goal, read it out loud and do Muscle Checking with a Partner, Self Muscle Checking or Noticing. Put a check mark on the line next to 1-6 if you are switched-off.

_____ 7. If you were switched-off for statement number 7 in Step 3-B above, which was "periodically re-evaluating your sales goals," then the action you should do now is to simply role play "re-evaluating." The way you can do this is to flip through this book, making believe it is your daily phone call log. As you flip through it, pretend that you are re-evaluating what you have been doing in terms of the goals you have set. For instance, if your goal was to average making twenty phone calls in a day and setting five appointments, in this role play you are flipping through to re-evaluate how well you are doing each day towards reaching this goal. (You can physically do this action or just pretend that you are doing it by visualizing it in your mind. The brain will register this action as if it was real.)

After completing this role play, immediately do Muscle Checking with a Partner, Self Muscle Checking, or Noticing. Put a check mark on the line next to 7 if you are switched-off.

_____ 8.    If you were switched-off for statement number 8 in Step 3-B above on keeping accurate records, the action you should do now is to simply role play record keeping. You can do this by making up some numbers and writing them on the Weekly Telephone Log chart below. Do this for twenty seconds or so.

After completing this role play, immediately do Muscle Checking with a Partner, Self Muscle Checking, or Noticing. Put a check mark on the line next to 8 if you are switched-off.

**Weekly Telephone Log**

|  | Monday | Tuesday | Wednesday | Thursday | Friday |
|---|---|---|---|---|---|
| Number of Calls Made | ЦН ЦНТ ЦНТ // | ЦНТ ЦНТ ЦНТ ЦНТ / | ЦНТ ЦНТ ЦНТ | ЦНТ ЦНТ ЦНТ ЦНТ | ЦНТ ЦНТ ЦНТ ЦНТ ЦНТ /// |

In the role play for record keeping, you are simply "pretending" that you have made a certain number of calls and are marking them off on this chart, as in the example above. Below is an empty chart for you to use.

|  | Monday | Tuesday | Wednesday | Thursday | Friday |
|---|---|---|---|---|---|
| Number of Calls Made |  |  |  |  |  |

_____ 9.    If you were switched-off for statement 9 in Step 3-B above on completing your goals in a timely manner, the action you should do now is to write a specific date when you are planning to complete a goal. After completing this role play, immediately do Muscle Checking with a Partner, Self Muscle Checking, or Noticing. Put a check mark next to 9 if you are switched-off.

## STEP 4. CHOOSING TO INCLUDE THE PAST:

In a moment you will be saying to yourself (or out loud to your partner, if you are working with a partner):

"My system now incorporates, in the most appropriate way, all relevant past events, known and unknown, into the Step 3 experience." (See page 45 for explanation for what "yes" or "no" means).

Now do Muscle Checking with a Partner, Self Muscle Checking, or Noticing.

**STEP 5. TAKING ACTION: Doing the Brain Gym Movements**

Now is the time to do the Brain Gym movements listed below.

- The Cross Crawl (see page 65)
- The Brain Buttons (see page 61)
- The Thinking Cap (see page 69)
- Lazy 8s (see page 63)
- Hook-ups (see page 63)
- The Positive Points (see page 69)
- Arm Activation (see page 60)
- Alphabet 8s (see page 59)
- The Double Doodle (see page 62)

**STEP 6. CHECKING THE CHANGES: Statements and Actions**

**Now you're going to repeat what was in Step 3. This time you should be switched-on for all of the Statements and Actions.**

**A. TONY'S STATEMENTS:**

Say out loud each of the TRIGGER STATEMENTS that you wrote and do Muscle Checking with a Partner, Self Muscle Checking, or Noticing for each one. You should now be switched-on for all of them.

**B. ASPECTS OF GOAL SETTING:**

Say the following statements out loud and then do Muscle Checking with a Partner, Self Muscle Checking, on Noticing. You should now be switched-on for all of them.

1. "I set personal goals."
2. "I set specific goals."
3. "I set positive goals."

4. "I set attainable and challenging goals."
5. "I set realistic goals."
6. "It's easy and natural to write my goals down."
7. "I periodically re-evaluate my sales goals."
8. "I keep accurate records on the selling process."
9. "I complete my goals in a timely manner."

**C. YOUR OWN ISSUES AND CHALLENGES:**
Do Muscle Checking with a Partner, Self Muscle Checking, or Noticing for each of your own statements (if you wrote any) for Step 3-C above. You should now be switched-on for all of them.

**D. ACTIONS:**
Now you will repeat the actions you were switched-off for in Step 3. Do each action for twenty seconds or so. This time when you do the action, you will find that you are switched-on and it's easier to do with less stress.

## STEP 7. WHERE ARE YOU NOW?

Now that you've completed the Balance for Goal Setting, it's time to reassess your level of improvement or change from your responses to the questionnaire on page 90. You'll find the statement that relates to this particular Balance below.

Place a check mark in the column that most clearly reflects your level of agreement or disagreement with the statement below. Now, turn to page 90 again to compare your initial response to your current response. Additionally, I urge you to mark your calendar and re-check your response a month from now to assess your continued improvement. Many people find that their improvement level has increased even more a month later.

|  |  | Strongly Agree | Agree | Doesn't Apply | Disagree | Strongly Disagree |
|---|---|---|---|---|---|---|
| 1. | I easily set sales goals for myself. |  |  |  |  |  |

## STEP 8. IT'S TIME TO CELEBRATE

If you're Self Muscle Checking or Noticing, congratulate yourself. If you're working with a partner, celebrate the successful completion of the Balance for Goal Setting and switching yourself on.

Enjoy your new state and your success in applying Tony's goal-setting tips and techniques to your sales life.

## STEP 9. REINFORCING THE BALANCE WITH HOME PLAY

Each time you finish reading and doing the Balances for the day, there's one more step before you end your Switched-On Selling session. Home play reinforces and enhances the re-wiring and rebalancing in the brain so the Balance will hold. Go to Chapter 14 on page 223 and follow the directions there.

**NOTE:** If you are continuing to work in this current session, skip this step and go on to the next chapter. Then turn to Reinforcing with Home Play after the last Balance.

# CHAPTER 8

# ENJOYING SELLING AS A PROFESSIONAL SALESPERSON

**Identifying Your Trigger Points:**

As you read through Tony's strategies in this chapter, you may want to write down any Trigger Points or Hot Button issues on page 128 as you go along. Or, if you prefer, you can read the entire chapter and then write your responses. Either way works just fine. (If necessary, review the instructions on Trigger Points on page 95.)

If you ask super-successful salespeople how they feel about their profession, it's likely that every single one of them will tell you they enjoy selling. In this chapter and the Balance that follows, we'll look at any issues that you might have relating to the profession, including the level of pride you have in your work and your motivation, confidence, resilience, and enthusiasm.

## Dealing with the Stereotypes

Are you comfortable with the title, "salesperson"? As professionals, we are well aware of the stereotyped image that salespeople have in our society. When you hear the word "salesperson" what descriptive words come to mind? Do you think of words like "courteous" "knowledgeable" "professional" and "helpful"? Or are you apt to think of "aggressive," "pushy," "persistent," and "pestering."

The truth of the matter is that even other salespeople don't like the image that salespeople have inherited—Willy Loman in *Death of a Salesman* or the used car dealer on Main Street. The fact that sales is so pervasive in all strata of society also helps explain why salespeople get such a bad rap. There are so MANY of us. We deal with salespeople virtually every day of our lives—from the insurance agent to the mechanic to the travel agent to the department store clerk.

Just as with other professionals, like the quack doctor or the crooked lawyer, you may interact with an unprofessional salesperson. Yet, you don't condemn ALL doctors and lawyers or judge them all according to a few negative experiences, do you? It stands to reason not to condemn all salespeople because of an unprofessional one here and there.

Another major reason that people have a bad image of salespeople is that too many of them receive inadequate or inappropriate training, or even worse, NO TRAINING at all. My introduction to sales is a classic example of this approach. I went to a Catholic grammar school, which undertook sales promotions each month as a way of generating money for school programs. I affectionately call it "the push of the month." Fortunately, I was from a big Italian Catholic family, so every month I outsold my classmates and every month I won the prize.

The point is that I heard repeatedly that I was a BORN salesman; I could sell anything to anybody; I had the gift of gab. This was my training ground and this is what I began to believe—that salespeople are born, not made; that you sell by telling and persuading, not by questioning, listening, and problem solving. Unfortunately, it's a myth that still persists in the profession today. It's no wonder that sales is misperceived, disrespected and misrepresented in the media and the arts.

Unfortunately, many sales training sessions focus on razzle-dazzle sales pitches, 101 closing techniques, or overcoming objections at all costs. This traditional approach has created the negative stereotypes that exist today. It is salesperson- rather than customer-oriented and tends to foster an "I win, you lose" attitude on the part of the seller.

The true sales professional knows a very different approach to sales. The underlying ethic for the professional or collaborative selling approach is that it's not so much WHAT you do as HOW you do it. It's not so much the business you are in as the WAY you are in business. The professional salesperson utilizes a philosophy that guides every aspect of his or her behavior and that naturally extends into their work. The entire approach is based on "non-manipulative" techniques, which create win/win situations for both buyer and seller every time, all the time. The cornerstone of this approach is the salesperson's desire to develop a long-term customer relationship rather than a one-shot sale. When sales is pursued with these perspectives and goals, it is a profession that can be enjoyed every single day.

The collaborative sales approach depends on several guiding principles:

1.  The sales process should be built around relationships that require openness and honesty on the part of both client and salesperson.

2.  People buy services or products most often because they feel understood by the seller—not because they were made to understand the product by an insistent salesperson.

3.  People strive for the right to make their own decisions, even if they are poor decisions. If YOU solve a problem for someone, they resent the solution. If you INFLICT the solution on them they resent you even if they accept the solution.

4.  If two people want to do business with each other, the details won't stop it from happening. If two people DON'T want to do business together, the details won't make it happen.

5.  It's not what you do that makes you a professional. It's HOW you do it.

6.  Prescription before diagnosis is malpractice. To paraphrase, presentation before information gathering is hucksterism.

The philosophy of the collaborative sales approach requires that we change the language of selling. Both the traditional and collaborative approaches to selling include four basic processes: information gathering, presentation, commitment, and follow-through. However, the emphasis on these steps varies greatly in the two approaches.

Collaborative Selling emphasizes the information gathering and follow-through stages; whereas traditional selling focuses on the pitch and closing techniques. Even the vernacular used in the traditional approach implies manipulation and superficiality, including phrases such as *overcoming objections, the pitch,* and *closing.* On the other hand, the terms we use in the non-manipulative approach show concern for the customer, as well as preparedness, cooperation, and the intent to continue the relationship after the sale is completed. These terms are *planning, meeting, studying, proposing, confirming,* and *assuring.*

The traditional approach is to grind the customer into submitting to the sale and to close, CLOSE, CLOSE! The real professional, however, takes more time to study the customer's problems and needs to propose relevant solutions and be of real service to their clients. Is it any wonder that professional salespeople are more successful than their high-pressure peers?

How does the professional become more successful? By paying attention to the key steps in the Collaborative Selling process.

1.  **Targeting:** This involves calling on the right people at the right time with the right product or service. Targeting is necessary to enter the sales call with the air of confidence and knowledge that is crucial to establishing a trust bond relationship. Without targeting, you may be pursuing the wrong kind of prospect at the wrong time.

2.  **Contacting:** The purpose here is to establish rapport with your client and to begin a business relationship. This is the time to prove your credibility and sincere desire to be of service. In developing trust with your clients, you will be able to elicit their real needs more easily.

3.  **Exploring:** The professional is truly concerned with the customer's needs and exhaustively studies the customer's situation. This occurs by encouraging the client to become involved in the sales process. By asking open-ended questions and listening attentively, the salesperson invites the customer to provide relevant information that otherwise would remain unknown. The client is then likely to feel that the sale is a mutual agreement rather than a manipulation by the seller.

4.  **Collaborating:** Unlike the traditional seller who gives an identical pitch to every client, the professional salesperson collaborates options and solutions with each individual client. This approach is more "know" than "show." The salesperson

knows what the client's needs are and seeks to satisfy them rather than putting on a show to dazzle and win the client over.

5. **Confirming:** Because the professional has taken an interest in the client's needs from the beginning, very little time needs to be spent hustling the close or overcoming objections. He doesn't need to focus on the close because the entire process has been an open discussion every step of the way. The confirming of the sale becomes much more a question of "when" rather than "if."

6. **Assuring:** The professional salesperson believes the sale truly begins when the customer says, "Yes." The salesperson and the client have made a commitment to continue a mutually beneficial relationship. The salesperson is responsible for her customers' satisfaction and maintains her business relationship with all her clients. She never lets that relationship fade. Assuring means the salesperson becomes the quality control person—making sure that the customer receives the proper order on the right delivery date, helping the client track results, and analyzing the effectiveness of the product for the problems that led to its purchase. By assuring customer satisfaction, the professional salesperson builds a clientele that will guarantee future sales and new prospects.

The collaborative approach guarantees that salespeople will not be regarded as a plague or pestilence, but as the professionals they really are.

## Sustaining Motivation

Not everyone can remain "up," optimistic, and energetic all the time. We all wax and wane in our moods, outlook, and energy levels. That's normal. People who are "up" most of the time have many methods to their madness. Adopt some of these methods to keep your motivation high:

**Do What You Love and the Money Will Follow.** Hopefully you love sales—the interactions with people, the challenges, the rewards, and the unlimited growth potential. Make time for what you love.

**Take Pride in What You Do, and It Will Have Meaning.** Even if you are starting at the bottom of the corporate ladder, do your job with pride and professionalism. Excellence is its own reward and will be recognized. Taking pride in doing the best job you can—no matter what the task—increases your self-esteem, competence, and sense of control over your life and work. Not to mention your promotability.

**Challenge Yourself with Continuous Self-Improvement.** Set realistic goals that are attainable in short periods of time. Break larger goals into smaller increments to give yourself frequent opportunities to experience a sense of accomplishment. Success feeds on success.

**Reward Yourself for Successes and Failures.** Salespeople are subjected to more than the average amount of rejection in their work, especially if they are cold calling on the phone. Devise ways to reward yourself for your efforts, even when you are not successful. Giving yourself an "E for Effort" will keep you going so that sooner or later you'll be rewarding yourself for a success. Remember that sales can be a numbers game, so every "no" brings you closer to a "yes."

**Think in Terms of a Career Path, Not Just a Job.** Commit yourself to doing the best job you can with your present company, but remember that few jobs last forever. Always keep your future destinations in mind while your eye is on the road immediately before you.

**Take Absolute Responsibility for Your Life and Career.** Realize that you and only you can shape your future. Again, small, positive steps lead to bigger and bigger payoffs.

## Confidence

Having confidence means you believe in yourself, you trust your own judgment and resourcefulness. In his many books on self-esteem, Dr. Nathaniel Branden defines self-esteem as the sum of self-confidence and self-respect. For him, self-confidence is knowing that you have the wherewithal to function reasonably well in the world. You feel competent to make choices, competent to satisfy your needs, to chart the course for your life. Having confidence in specific situations, such as in gaining influence with someone, would flow from a general self-confidence about your ability to meet life's challenges.

A person who exhibits confidence appreciates a sincere compliment and doesn't brush it off. A confident person is comfortable giving, and receiving, compliments. He's also able to handle criticism if it comes his way because he basically likes himself and knows that a single negative incident won't change that.

Confidence in yourself gets built up over time. You can fake confidence, and you may need to at first, but real self-confidence comes from a history of small victories and accomplishments that add up to a sense that you can handle yourself well in most every situation. I suggest you take an inventory of the major accomplishments you've achieved over the past few years. Then remind yourself of the minor ones too. What about the computer course you completed? Have you built anything that is still standing? What about those kids you're raising? That's (!) an accomplishment. Don't be modest. Tell the truth about how hard you worked, what sacrifices you've made. If you can't think of any, then begin by congratulating yourself for living as long as you have. Sheer survival is an accomplishment these days! Seriously, it pays to take the time to know your strengths and appreciate them. What's unique about you? What skills do you bring to an organization or project that you can count on?

Confidence is a fundamental trait for flexibility. It's hard to be flexible when you're fearful or easily intimidated. Confidence is indispensable if you want to engage someone's attention.

## Positiveness

Positiveness means maintaining a state of positive expectations about people and situations, including a positive state of energy in your thoughts and emotional patterns. Dr. Norman Vincent Peale's book, *The Power of Positive Thinking,* was published almost sixty years ago, and it continues to sell well because it contains such a universal truth that the attitudes we hold help to shape the reality we experience.

Having a positive attitude isn't something you just tack on to your old personality. That positiveness isn't external like a new suit. It comes from deep within you. It has to, or it would get wiped out with the first sign of a countervailing negative force. Positiveness is built on knowing what strengths you have and on surrounding yourself with other sources of positiveness.

This involves taking a personal inventory about your talents and skills and also what you like to do. Ideally, we'd all like to make a living, or spend our time doing what we love. The people who come the closest to that are those who actually take the time to figure out what they love doing. Then you figure out what skills you have and which ones you need and take a step closer to matching your ideal life's work with the reality of your work life.

Knowing what strengths you have to build on will only get you so far. The second aspect of positiveness is surrounding yourself with other sources of the same energy. Occasionally we hear stories of people who struggle against great odds, prove the naysayers wrong, and achieve the nearly impossible. They turn around a defunct company, they stop a highway from going through virgin land, they bring out a new product line in record time, or they beat the odds on terminal cancer.

By definition, they had to know what they could do themselves and what they needed to get from others. Those stories rarely mention the fact that those people always had some other source of positive energy outside themselves that kept them going. Most probably it was other people they could rely on for support or other people who were also positive about their ability to succeed. Perhaps they were also motivated by the example of some historical figure. Perhaps they drew strength from a spiritual source. The point is they didn't do it alone. They needed to be embedded in some sort of supportive, positive context that recharged them when their own batteries were running low.

Ideally, you surround yourself with the kinds of people who exhibit the positive traits we're talking about. Avoid the two-dimensional folks who tend toward the negative traits we discussed earlier—the ones who see things as either/or, right or wrong, and don't care to entertain any other thoughts. These people don't help recharge you; they drain you.

## Resilience

Resilience means knowing how to cope in spite of setbacks, or barriers, or limited resources. Resilience is a measure of how much you want something and how much you're willing, and able, to overcome obstacles to get it. It has to do with your emotional strength. For instance, how many cold calls can you make in a row that all turn out to be "no thank you?"

Remember Abraham Lincoln? You wouldn't, if he had given up. In 1832 he was defeated for the state legislature. Then he was elected to it in 1834. In 1838 he was defeated for speaker of the state house. In 1840 he was defeated for elector. Lincoln ran for Congress in 1843 and guess what—he was defeated. He was elected to Congress in '46 and then lost for re-election in '49. He ran for U.S. Senate in 1855 and— was defeated. In '56 he was defeated for Vice-President. He ran again for the U.S. Senate in 1858 and lost. And in 1860, Abraham Lincoln was elected president of the United States—one of the best ones we've ever had. That's resilience!

Your challenge to stay resilient may not be quite the size of Abe Lincoln's. You might be working on making a sales quota when 90 percent of your prospects say "no." You might be pushing for a change in a local zoning ordinance, and you have to fight city hall. You might be trying to get your co-workers to recycle paper to save money and trees. When you're up against obstacles you can either maintain your resilience, or cave in to defeat.

## Enthusiasm

You generally wear your positiveness "inside." But your enthusiasm is how you show it to the world by your face, your voice, and your gestures. Sometimes we *feel* enthusiastic about our ideas but we're afraid to show it. But I think the people who influence us the most are those who are able to express on the outside what they're feeling on the inside.

A friend of mine remembers touring a client's office and seeing "cute" signs with negative messages plastered everywhere: "It's hard to soar like an eagle when you're surrounded by turkeys," "Even a bad day on vacation is better than a good day at work," and the like. Every message that every employee saw every day was negative. No wonder, my friend later concluded, morale there was so low.

Most people like to be around those who radiate joy and interest, whether at work or at play. What's more, enthusiasm is infectious. It spreads. But so does the lack of it. The choice is yours.

We've probably all worked with people who were negative about the job, the firm, their colleagues, the environment, the world itself, and then were further upset when—surprise! —they didn't get the big promotion. They chose to be problems, not problem-solvers. So was it any wonder that the boss would pick someone who was more positive and enthusiastic?

The response you receive from the world is in large measure a reflection of your own attitude. From the beginning to the end of every meeting with another person, you are on stage: You're being evaluated by that other person, consciously or subconsciously. While I'm not suggesting you put on a phony happy-face, I am reminding you to be aware that your every word, gesture, expression, and impression is being watched—especially in initial encounters—and will either help or hinder you in fostering honest, open, and trusting communications.

If your overall approach is cheerful, hopeful, and tolerant of differences, you send out a positive message. On the other hand, if you're critical, pessimistic, and intolerant of anything unfamiliar, you convey a negative outlook. Guess which attitude gets better results when you're trying to influence people?

---

# BALANCE FOR ENJOYING SELLING

This Balance is designed to switch you on to enjoy being a professional salesperson. In this Balance, Step 5, the Taking Action Step uses the Dennison Laterality Repatterning (DLR). Let me give you some history. Years ago researchers Dolman and Delacatto found that when children with learning disabilities did The Cross Crawl along the floor, their grades improved. (See The Cross Crawl on page 65.) However, when this work started to spread into school systems, teachers reported mixed results. It worked with some of the children but not with others. It turns out that some children were actually switched-off for The Cross Crawl. In other words, The Cross Crawl has a positive effect for some children but not for others. Those who were not switched-on for The

Cross Crawl were operating homolaterally, meaning that only one side of the brain was operating at a time, instead of both sides. Research by Dr. Paul Dennison indicated that this homolateral brain functioning contributed to their learning disabilities.

Again, it was Dr. Dennison's work that created a breakthrough when he developed the method that became known as Dennison Laterality Repatterning (DLR). After doing DLR, those who were previously switched-off for The Cross Crawl were now switched-on. Finally, by incorporating DLR, the positive benefits of The Cross Crawl became accessible to everyone.

A research study that measured motor coordination skills in students showed the positive impact of hemisphere integration using DLR used in the Brain Gym process. In this study the students were divided into three groups. The control group did nothing and, at the end of the study, their motor coordination skills were unchanged. The second group of students did a series of Brain Gym movements and exercises for five minutes each day. At the end of the study, this group showed a statistically significant improvement in their motor coordination abilities. The third group did DLR just once, at the very beginning of the study, and then every day they did the same Brain Gym movements and exercises as the second group. The only thing different between these two groups was that one group had done DLR one time. At the end of the study, the group that did the DLR had a rate of improvement more than double that of the second group, indicating that DLR has a profound impact on brain integration. (This study is available at www.Teplitz.com/BrainGymResearch.htm.)

Why is DLR so helpful? Let's use the analogy of high gear and low gear responses from the body. An example of a high gear response is when you're driving your car on the interstate. If traffic is light, driving doesn't take a lot of effort or energy, and you make really good time. It's so easy, and you can cover a great distance in a shorter time frame. That's the high gear concept. An example of low gear is when you come to an accident or a lane closure due to road construction as you are driving. It's a new and unfamiliar situation. You have to slow down to figure out what to do next. This situation requires a homolateral response, with each hemisphere of the brain firing independently of the other.

The ideal is to have both hemispheres of the brain firing and communicating easily and effectively. When you pass by the situation on the highway, you easily move right back into high gear and, once again, you are cruising along. This is what is called *integrated* high and low gear.

What I'm looking for you to achieve is to have your body automatically function from the highest state of integration. This will allow you to easily stop and clearly think when you're in a new selling situation, as well as access your natural selling skills. This integrated state allows you to move quickly and efficiently from the whole picture, which is the completed sale, to the individual parts of the selling process—without getting stuck in one or the other.

When you are cruising along as a successful and effective salesperson, you are in integrated high gear, which feels natural, effortless, and easy since it is based on a process you have learned well. Then, when you encounter a new selling situation, you will be able to momentarily pause, think, and creatively meet this new challenge. The ability to do this is called integrated low gear. When you come to a new sales situation, integrated low gear allows you to gear down at the appropriate moment. Then, as soon as you've mastered the new situation, you are able to easily and effortlessly switch back to being in high gear.

The Balance that follows will allow you to experience the impact of Dennison Laterality Repatterning so you can experience the change at a very deep level in terms of the selling process. Your feelings and attitudes about selling will be enhanced and uplifted. In addition, by switching you on for The Cross Crawl, you will also be switched-on for all of the Brain Gym movements and exercises. This means that any of these movements and exercises that you do in the other Balances will have an even more positive impact on you.

## STEP 1. TRIGGER POINTS:

Identify the Trigger Points that came up for you in this chapter and write them down. Does anything that you've just read act as a "Hot Button issue" for you? For instructions see page 85 in the Balance for Positive Selling.

| TRIGGER POINTS | POSITIVE GOAL STATEMENTS |
|---|---|
|  |  |
|  |  |
|  |  |
|  |  |
|  |  |

**STEP 2. CALIBRATION: Preparing for the Process**

If necessary, refer to the more detailed instructions on Calibration on page 71.

1. **Need for Water:** To make sure you are not dehydrated, drink some water.
2. **Electrical Circuitry:** To make sure your electrical circuitry is operating efficiently, do The Brain Buttons (page 61).
3. **Activating:** To make sure your body is ready to move, do The Cross Crawl (page 65).
4. **Stress Reduction:** To make sure your stress response is deactivated, do Hook-ups (page 63).
5. **Method to Use:** Select whether you will do Muscle Checking with a Partner, Self Muscle Checking, or Noticing (page 54).

6. **"Yes"/"No" Response:** Use the biofeedback response method you chose to ask your body for a "yes" and then a "no" response (page 45).

**NOTE:** When you are in the middle of a Balance, it's possible you may begin to get inaccurate or questionable results. While this rarely occurs, it is a possibility. In case it does occur, simply repeat the Calibration procedure, and then proceed with the Balance, beginning at the point where you began to experience the inaccurate or questionable results.

**STEP 3. CHECKING THE ISSUES: Statements and Actions**

　　A. **TRIGGER POINTS:** If you wrote down any statements from Tony's material, do Muscle Checking with a Partner, Self Muscle Checking, or Noticing on both the negative goal side and the positive goal side of what you wrote. If you are Muscle Checking with a Partner, read the statements out loud. You should be switched-off for both. If you are not switched-off, then what you thought was a negative Trigger Point is not one.

　　B. **ASPECTS OF ENJOYING SELLING:** Make the following statement and do Muscle Checking with a Partner, Self Muscle Checking, or Noticing to determine if your body is switched-on or off after saying the statement. If you are Muscle Checking with a Partner, read it out loud. Place a check mark next to the statement if you are switched-off.

　　　　_____ 1. "I am an effective and successful salesperson. I enjoy what I do and feel good about it."

　　C. **YOUR OWN ISSUES AND CHALLENGES:** Write your own positive affirmations if there are still aspects of Enjoying Selling that you still feel are an issue or challenge for you. While you have written those as positive statements, you should be switched-off when you do Muscle Checking with a Partner, Self Muscle Checking, or Noticing because your brain is not yet switched-on for achieving it. It is also okay not have to have any statements that you want to add.

_____ 2. _____

_____ 3. _____

If you had no Trigger Points and were also switched-on for all of these statements in 3-B and C, then that means you don't have any major issues or difficulties with this aspect of the selling process. If this is the case, skip to Step 5. By doing the DLR, you can still expand these aspects of the sales process that are already positive for you to an even higher level of success.

> **D. ACTION:**
>
> Now do a physical action, role play, or visualization for twenty seconds or so for each of the Trigger Points and/or Statements above in Step 3-B and C for which you were switched-off. Do each action for 20 seconds or so and then do Muscle Checking with a Partner, Self Muscle Checking, or Noticing after the action. For Step 3-B and C put a check mark on the line next to each action for which you were switched-off.
>
> (See page 106 in the Balance for Goal Setting if you need further explanation of this step.)

**STEP 4. CHOOSING TO INCLUDE THE PAST:**

> In a moment you will be saying to yourself (or out loud to your partner, if you are working with a partner):
>
> "My system now incorporates, in the most appropriate way, all relevant past events, known and unknown, into the Step 3 experience."
>
> (See page 45 for an explanation of a "yes" or "no" response). Now do Muscle Checking with a Partner, Self Muscle Checking, or Noticing.

**STEP 5. TAKING ACTION: Dennison Laterality Repatterning**

> Turn to page 134 to do the Dennison Laterality Repatterning

(DLR). Once you finish the Dennison Laterality Repatterning, go on to Step 6 below.

## STEP 6. CHECKING THE CHANGES AFTER DOING THE DLR:

Now you will repeat the Statements and Actions you did in Step 3 above. Again, do an action for each of the Statements and Actions for which you were switched-off when you first did them in Step 3. This time when you do them, you may find that it's easier to do with less stress.

### A. TRIGGER POINTS:

Say out loud each of the Positive Goal Statements you wrote and do Muscle Checking with a Partner, Self Muscle Checking, or Noticing for each one. You should now be switched-on for all of them.

### B. ASPECT OF ENJOYING SELLING:

Say the following statement out loud and then do Muscle Checking with a Partner, Self Muscle Checking, or Noticing. You should now be switched-on for it.

"I am an effective and successful salesperson. I enjoy what I do and feel good about it."

### C. YOUR OWN ISSUES AND CHALLENGES:

Do Muscle Checking with a Partner, Self Muscle Checking, or Noticing for each of your own statements (if you wrote any) for Step 3 above. You should now be switched-on for all of them.

### D. ACTIONS:

Now you will repeat the actions you were switched-off for in Step 3 above, again doing each of them for twenty seconds or so. This time when you do the action, you will find that you are switched-on and it's easier to do with less stress.

## STEP 7. WHERE ARE YOU NOW?

Now that you've completed the Balance for Enjoying Selling, it's time to reassess your level of improvement or change from your responses to the questionnaire on page 90. You'll find the questions that relate to this particular Balance below.

Place a check mark in the column that most clearly reflects your level of agreement or disagreement with each statement below. Now, turn to page 90 again to compare your initial response to your current response. Additionally, I urge you to mark your calendar and re-check your responses a month from now to assess your continued improvement. Many people find that their improvement level has increased even more a month later.

| | | Strongly Agree | Agree | Doesn't Apply | Disagree | Strongly Disagree |
|---|---|---|---|---|---|---|
| 2. | I enjoy selling. | | | | | |
| 3. | I am effective as a salesperson. | | | | | |
| 4. | I view myself as a successful salesperson. | | | | | |

## STEP 8. IT'S TIME TO CELEBRATE

If you're Self Muscle Checking or Noticing, congratulate yourself. If you're working with a partner, celebrate the successful completion of the Balance for Enjoying Selling.

## STEP 9. REINFORCING THE BALANCE WITH HOME PLAY

Each time you finish reading and doing the Balances for the day, there's one more step before you end your Switched-On Selling session. Home play reinforces and enhances the re-wiring and rebalancing in the brain so the Balance will hold. Go to Chapter 14 on page 223 and follow the directions there.

**NOTE:** If you are continuing to work in this current session, skip this step and go on to the next chapter. Then turn to Reinforcing with Home Play after the last Balance.

# DENNISON LATERALITY REPATTERNING

*Dennison Laterality Repatterning integrates the left and right sides of the body and brain.*

## STEP 1. PRE-ACTIVITIES:

Do each activity and do Muscle Checking with a Partner, Self Muscle Checking, or Noticing. Note whether you are switched-on or off for each activity and mark each result in the right-hand column. After you do the Pre-Activities, I'll tell you what the responses should be. If you're not having these responses, don't be concerned, as that's what doing the DLR will change.

| | |
|---|---|
| • **The Cross Crawl** Do a half dozen Cross Crawls. Then do Muscle Checking with a Partner, Self Muscle Checking, or Noticing to learn whether you are switched-on or off. Mark your response for each part of Step 1 in the column to the right. | Switched: On___ Off___  |
| • **Homolateral Crawl** As if you are a puppet on a string, raise the right arm and the right leg up at the same time. Then, after lowering the right arm and leg, raise the left arm and leg up at the same time. Repeat six times. Then do Muscle Checking with a Partner, Self Muscle Checking, or Noticing to learn whether you are switched-on or switched off. Mark your response. | Switched: On___ Off___  |

| | |
|---|---|
| • **Close your eyes and visualize the letter "X."** <br> Do Muscle Checking with a Partner, Self Muscle Checking, or while you continue to visualize the "X" to learn whether you are switched-on or off and mark your response. | Switched: On___ Off___ <br>  |
| • **Close your eyes and visualize two parallel lines.** <br> You can think of railroad tracks. Do Muscle Checking with a Partner, Self Muscle Checking, or Noticing while you continue to visualize the parallel lines to learn whether you are switched-on or off. Mark your response. | Switched: On___ Off___ <br> 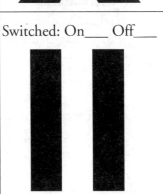 |

**The results you are looking for are:**
- Switched-on for The Cross Crawl
- Switched-off for the Homolateral Crawl
- Switched-on for the X
- Switched-off for the parallel lines

As I said before, if your results are a different pattern of "on" and "off," don't be concerned because that's what we are going to change by the end of the Dennison Laterality Repatterning. This means at the end of this Balance, your results will be appropriate.

**STEP 2. STARTING THE PROCESS**

In starting the Dennison Laterality Repatterning process, you will be doing The Cross Crawl while looking diagonally up to the left and right with just your eyes. You will also be humming a steady note while you first look diagonally up in each direction. The humming is done as a part of this process because we want to keep your logical mind, your left hemisphere, from getting involved in the process. By humming a steady note while doing The Cross Crawl, you are activating the right hemisphere so that this movement will become your body's natural reflex.

Let's do it now:

**Repatterning**

1. Do fifteen to twenty of The Cross Crawls while looking diagonally up to the left, keeping your nose facing forward and, at the same time, humming a steady note. Next do fifteen to twenty of The Cross Crawls while looking diagonally up to the right, keeping your nose facing forward and again, at the same time, humming a steady note. Remember to keep your nose pointed straight ahead so only your eyes are looking diagonally up. Do the movements slowly.

2. You are now ready to do the Homolateral Crawl while counting out loud for fifteen to twenty complete repetitions while keeping your nose facing forward. (A complete repetition is raising the arm and leg of one side up and down and then the other side up and down.) This time you will be looking diagonally down with just your eyes. First look to the right for fifteen to twenty repetitions and then repeat the Homolateral Crawl fifteen to twenty more times while looking down to the left and counting out loud. Do the movements slowly.

## STEP 3. INTEGRATION METAPHOR

Hold your arms out to each side as if you are showing someone that you caught a big fish. Close your eyes and visualize holding the left hemisphere of your brain in your left hand and the right hemisphere of your brain in your right hand. Once you have both hemispheres clearly visualized, begin to physically bring your hands together slowly while you continue to visualize your hemispheres coming together.

When your hands meet, intertwine or interlace your fingers. Finally, move your hands to your chest and put a slight pressure on your palms while you feel both sides of your brain coming together. Hold this position for ten or fifteen seconds or longer if you want to. When you are done, release your hands. (See Illustration 00)

## STEP 4. CEMENTING IN THE CROSS CRAWL CHANGES

This part of the process cements in the changes you just made. Keeping your nose facing straight ahead, do The Cross Crawl for approximately thirty seconds, while you are rotating your eyes in circles. First rotate several times in one direction and then rotate them several times in the opposite direction. You don't have to count the exact number of times. (And, no, you don't hum this time.)

## STEP 5. CEMENTING IN THE HOMOLATERAL CRAWL CHANGES

Keeping your nose facing straight ahead, do the Homolateral Crawl for approximately thirty seconds, while you are rotating your eyes in a circle. First rotate several times in one direction and then do it several times in the opposite direction. (You don't have to count this time.)

## STEP 6. POST ACTIVITIES

You are now going to repeat each of the pre-activities that you did in Step 1. Do each action and then do Muscle Checking with a Partner, Self Muscle Checking, or Noticing after doing each of the following:

- Do six of The Cross Crawls. Do Muscle Checking with a Partner, Self Muscle Checking, or Noticing and you should be switched-on.
- Do six Homolateral Crawls. Do Muscle Checking with a Partner, Self Muscle Checking, or Noticing and you should be switched-off.

- Visualize the letter "X." Do Muscle Checking with a Partner, Self Muscle Checking, or Noticing and you should be switched-on.
- Visualize two parallel lines. Do Muscle Checking with a Partner, Self Muscle Checking, or Noticing and you should be switched-off.

The DLR has integrated the left and right sides of the body and brain, resulting in the appropriate responses to these activities. You are now switched-on to be able to naturally experience the Integrated High Gear state while you also have access to the Integrated Low Gear ability to momentarily pause and think clearly in new selling situations.

**STEP 7. FINISHING UP THE DLR**
End by doing The Cross Crawl again six more times while visualizing an "X."

**STEP 8. Return to Step 6 of the Balance for Enjoying Selling on page 132 and do the rest of the steps.**

# CHAPTER 9

# PLANNING FOR SALES CALLS

**Identifying Your Trigger Points:**

As you read through Tony's strategies in this chapter, you may want to write down any Trigger Points or Hot Button issues on page 145 as you go along. Or, if you prefer, you can read the entire chapter and then write your responses. Either way works just fine. (If necessary, review the instructions on Trigger Points on page 95.)

Being fully prepared for the sales interview has a number of advantages for both you and the customer. By being prepared, you are better able to react to the demands of the sales transaction. You can talk about those service benefits that relate directly to the needs of the buyer. You can bring the proper materials to the interview so that it progresses smoothly and efficiently. This saves time for the buyer because he is not burdened by an inefficient interview or salesperson. You are able to set realistic call objectives and develop a sales strategy around them. You impress the buyer with your knowledge, preparation, strategy, and confidence. In other words, preparing for sales interviews leads to more, bigger, and better sales. It spells success!

Having a sales plan for each customer is nothing more than *selling by objectives*. You should plan before entering a sales situation, rather than reacting to whatever develops in the sales interview. This is not to say that if you preplan you can do without the skills necessary to spot a situation and react quickly. The chances of selling success are much greater if selling instincts are combined with preparation.

Planning a sales presentation involves nothing more than using common sales sense. You have something to offer your prospects that either provides them a benefit or helps them prevent a loss. Therefore, you plan before the presentation to gear everything you say to achieve either or both of those two objectives.

Obviously, you should know all you can about the prospects upon whom you are calling. Unless you know, you cannot hope to hold their attention to what you have to say. Figuratively, you must "walk in their shoes." You must relate what you say to their needs, their desires, and their objectives.

Get to know the real decision maker, along with those who can influence the ultimate decision, within the prospect's company. This vital information should be ascertained as soon as possible. In addition, what is the purchase decision process? Does an individual make the purchase commitment or does a committee do it? If an individual can make the purchase decision, can she make it only up to a certain dollar amount? Are there any external influences on the decision process, such as attorneys, accountants, consultants, or business advisors?

Your primary activity in preparing for a sales call will be research. You'll want to know whom to contact, their possible needs, their financial status, when they may want to buy, and who your competitors are. If you're well organized, this task will be far easier. Be sure to take advantage of your company as a source of information. Your prospect may be a former or present client of your company. In this case, a file will already exist which can provide all the information you need.

The more information you have about a prospect, the better your chances of making a sale. Some basic areas need to be explored as part of your pre-call homework. These are covered step by step in the following sections.

## Who is the Decision Maker?

When you make your sales call you don't want to waste your time. It is imperative that you meet with someone who is in a decision-making position. This person must also be knowledgeable enough to know what you are talking about. If you discover that this person does not have the authority to buy or to make decisions, you must diplomatically find out how the system works or whom you must see. Some company structures require the completion of a long chain of events before a decision can be made. If this is the case, ask your prospect, "Would you give me an idea of your company's decision-making process for a purchase such as this?" If that process involves more than one person seeing your presentation, try to arrange to show everyone at once. In some cases, however, it will be necessary for you to show several people your product at different times.

## What is the Climate of Your Prospect's Business?

To get a feel for the climate of your prospect's business, you need to ask some general questions. You might start off by suggesting, "Tell me a little bit about your business." This is a safe, non-threatening opener which can lead the way to more in-depth probing such as "What's happening with sales?" or "Are you encountering any special problems with your present product or service?" You'll need to adapt these questions to your industry, however. You can see that some delicate probing can identify needs that might otherwise have remained hidden.

Aside from making money, what are they trying to accomplish in business? Forget about your product or service for a moment and get a grasp of the overall picture. Once you understand a company's primary purpose in the marketplace, you'll be able to relate to it in a more relevant way. This will also show them that you are interested in their business and well-being in addition to making sales.

Once you determine your prospect's current situation and goals and objectives, you can readily determine if a "need gap" exists. A need gap exists when the prospect's current situation is not living up to or accomplishing his desired situation (objectives or end results). The greater the need gap, the greater and more immediate the need for the prospect to change what he's currently doing or purchasing. The greater the need gap, the greater the probability for you to make a sale.

You might also think about what the consequences could be if they don't use your product or service. Having that insight, you can develop some very strong and persuasive selling points to use in your presentation.

## What are Your Call Objectives?

Every time you see a client, you should have a reason for making that call. Dropping by to say hello is nice, but may be a waste of time. If you want to be sociable, you can use the phone. If you haven't sold the prospect yet, your reason for stopping by should be one of the action steps that will move you closer to making the sale. For example, you might stop by to show the prospect the latest in your product line or a new service you have to offer. Each time you see your prospect you should try to learn more about his or her needs. Ideally, each call will produce tangible evidence that you are making progress with the prospect; otherwise, you're just going through the motions.

Although it is not generally advisable to have specifically worded questions that you will ask in a particular sequence, it is advisable to have a questioning strategy. This simply means that you should have a general idea of what you would like to ask to get the particular information you require.

## What are the Decision-Making Criteria?

Part of your research should uncover the reason(s) why your prospect might be interested in your product or service. This is almost independent of need. You've already established or suspect a strong need, but why is that need present?

Once you have this information, you can look for the criteria used by each person you speak to in the company. In general you know that an executive will be interested in the long-term goals of the company or in increasing overall sales and profits. A middle manager will base his opinion on the cost effectiveness of your product while the first-line supervisors will be concerned with installation and operation.

When you contact each of these individuals, be aware of their different perspectives and gear your presentation to the criteria upon which their decision will be based. Everyone wants to know if the purchase will benefit him or her. If you can show everyone along the line that they, too, will benefit, then you'll be a strong contender in the race for their business.

After you've presented your ideas and created some interest, many prospects will want you to prove your claims. They may ask you for a demonstration or an opportunity to try out the product in their business. An easier and less time-consuming way to prove your product or service is to offer testimonials from people the prospects know and trust.

If you can find out in advance what means will be necessary to prove yourself, you can spend time preparing to make your proof effective and appropriate to your prospect's needs.

## What Is Your Competitive Edge?

Is there something about you that is unique? Something that gives you the advantage over other companies and salespeople? If so, use it to your advantage. Often a minor detail will tip the balance in your direction. Many sales have been made based on the statement, "In addition to the product, you also get me. I come with the package. I'll be here when you need me to make sure that everything runs smoothly and that you realize the full benefits of the product." That kind of enthusiasm and sincerity makes salespeople winners!

During your presentation, highlight your unique selling factors. This is an excellent time to admit a limitation in your product. The customer will find out about it anyway, so you might as well score some points by being the one to enlighten him or her. When pointing out a weak point, contrast it with a strong point. For example, if you're selling stand-alone scanners, say, "Yet, it's true that my XYZ scanner does not also make copies, fax or print from a computer like a multi-function printer, copier, scanner, fax machine. The XYZ scanner, however, copies 30 pages at a time, both sides, in an automatic sheet feeder in a PDF file that is 10% of the KB size of scans from a multi-function machine. That makes your scanning jobs simpler, faster and much easier to store and email because of its much smaller KB size."

When you're rehearsing your presentation, either with someone or in your mind, try imagining what the prospect's reactions will be. What questions will be asked? What resistance will you encounter from skeptical people? If you know the potential objections and questions, then you have time to prepare yourself.

## What Commitment Will You Ask For?

It is essential, at the end of a sales call, to know what action will follow. The only way to know this is to confirm it with the prospect in the form of a verbal agreement. There are all kinds of things you might ask for: more information, a referral, permission to give a demonstration, or, best of all, for the order itself!

Regardless of the commitment you seek, before you make the call you should have in mind a specific end result for the meeting. This is the most important part of your call objective.

Many products, such as computers, serve different functions for different clients. If your product or service falls into this category how will you know if it is benefiting the client or not? You know some of the improvements he or she wants to make, but you can't know them all. So ask your client, "What are the criteria that you will use to judge the effectiveness of this product?" Your client will tell you what they are looking for and when they hope to see results.

There's an old adage—"If you fail to plan, then you are planning to fail." In sales, this couldn't be truer. Your research and preparation will educate you so that you *will* be of service to your client. If you don't prepare yourself, you might as well be calling everyone cold without even knowing their names. It's not a very attractive alternative. Preparation and planning are like studying a map: You'll know which road to take with your prospect to get where you *both* want to go.

---

# BALANCE FOR PLANNING
# THE SALES CALL

*In this Balance, we will be working on your confidence and preparedness level in getting ready to approach potential clients and customers.*

### STEP 1. TRIGGER POINTS:

We're now going to give you the opportunity to identify the Trigger Points that came up for you in this chapter and write them down. Does anything that you've just read act as a "Hot Button issue" for you? If you need an explanation of Trigger Points, go to page 95.

| TRIGGER POINTS | POSITIVE GOAL STATEMENTS |
|---|---|
|  |  |
|  |  |
|  |  |
|  |  |
|  |  |

## STEP 2. CALIBRATION: Preparing for the Process

If necessary, refer to the more detailed instructions on Calibration on page 71.

1. **Need for Water:** To make sure you are not dehydrated, drink some water.

2. **Electrical Circuitry:** To make sure your electrical circuitry is operating efficiently, do The Brain Buttons (page 61).

3. **Activating:** To make sure your body is ready to move, do The Cross Crawl (page 65).

4. **Stress Reduction:** To make sure your stress response is deactivated, do Hook-ups (page 63).

5. **Method to Use:** Select whether you will do Muscle Checking with a Partner, Self Muscle Checking, or Noticing (page 54).

6. **"Yes"/"No" Response:** Use the biofeedback response method you chose to ask your body for a "yes" and then a "no" response (page 45).

**NOTE:** When you are in the middle of a Balance, it's possible you may begin to get inaccurate or questionable results. While this rarely occurs, it is a possibility. In case it does occur, simply repeat the Calibration procedure, and then proceed with the Balance, beginning at the point where you began to experience the inaccurate or questionable results.

## STEP 3. CHECKING THE ISSUES: Statements and Actions

### A. TRIGGER POINTS:

If you wrote down any statements from Tony's material, do Muscle Checking with a Partner, Self Muscle Check or Notice on both the negative side and the positive goal side of what you wrote. If you are Muscle Checking with a Partner, read the statements out loud. You should be switched-off for both. If you are not switched-off, then what you thought was a negative Trigger Point is not one.

### B. ASPECTS OF PLANNING:

Make the following statements one at a time and do Muscle Checking with a Partner, Self Muscle Checking, or Noticing to determine if your body is switched-on or off after saying each statement. If you are Muscle Checking with a Partner, read it out loud. Place a check mark next to any statements for which you are switched-off.

____ 1. "I feel positive, comfortable, and confident about approaching customers about my products or services."

____ 2. "I choose to make sales calls."

____ 3. "I effectively collect data and research on a potential client before I make the sales call."

____ 4. "I easily and comfortably surf the Web."

### C. YOUR OWN ISSUES AND CHALLENGES:

Write your own positive affirmations if there are aspects of planning for sales calls that still are an issue or challenge for you. After you have written those statements, you should be switched-off when you do Muscle Checking with a Partner, Self Muscle Checking or Noticing. It is okay not have to have any statements that you want to add.

_____ 5. _____

_____ 6. _____

If you were switched-on for all of these statements, it means you don't have any major issues or difficulties with this aspect of the selling process. If this is the case, skip to Step 5 and do the Brain Gym movements and exercises in that step. By doing the Brain Gym exercises and movements, you can expand aspects of the sales process that are already positive for you and move them to an even higher level of success.

### D. ACTIONS:

Now do a physical action, role play, or visualization for twenty seconds or so for each of the Trigger Points and the statements you placed a check mark next to in Step 3-B and C for which you were switched-off. Do Muscle Checking with a Partner, Self Muscle Checking, or Noticing for each action as soon as you complete it. Place a check mark next to each action for which you are also switched-off.

## STEP 4. CHOOSING TO INCLUDE THE PAST:

In a moment you will be saying to yourself (or out loud to your partner, if you are working with a partner):

"My system now incorporates, in the most appropriate way, all relevant past events, known and unknown, into the Step 3 experience."

**147**

(See page 45 for explanation for what a "yes" or "no" mean). Now do Muscle Checking with a Partner, Self Muscle Checking, or Noticing.

**STEP 5. TAKING ACTION: Doing the Brain Gym Movements**
Now is the time to do the Brain Gym Movements listed below:
- The Cross Crawl (see page 65)
- Water (simply drink a glass of water.)
- Belly Breathing (see page 61)
- Hook-ups (see page 63)
- The Positive Points (see page 69)
- Brain Buttons (see page 61)
- Earth Buttons (see page 62)
- Space Buttons (see page 64)
- Lazy 8s (see page 63)

**STEP 6. CHECKING THE CHANGES: Statements and Actions**
Now you're going to repeat Step 3. This time you should be switched-on for all of the Statements and Actions.
**A. TRIGGER POINTS:**
Say out loud, each of the TRIGGER STATEMENTS that you wrote and do Muscle Checking with a Partner, Self Muscle Checking, or Noticing for each one. You should now be switched-on for all of them.
**B. ASPECTS OF PLANNING:**
Say the following statements out loud and then do Muscle Checking with a Partner, Self Muscle Checking, or Noticing. You should now be switched-on for all of them.
1. "I feel positive, comfortable, and confident about approaching customers about my products or services."
2. "I choose to make sales calls."
3. "I effectively collect data and research on a potential client before I make the sales call."

4. "I easily and comfortably do research by surfing the web."

C. **YOUR OWN ISSUES AND CHALLENGES:** If you wrote any of your own statements in Step 3-C, read them now. Do Muscle Checking with a Partner, Self Muscle Checking, or Noticing for each one. You should now be switched-on for every one of them.

If you had no Trigger Points and were switched-on for all of the Statements in 3B and 3C, that means you don't have any major issues with this aspect of the selling process. If this is the case, skip to Step 5 and do the Brain Gym movements and exercises to move yourself to an even higher level of success.

D. **ACTIONS:**

Now you will repeat the actions you were switched-off for in Step 3 above, again doing each of them for twenty seconds or so. This time when you do the action, you will find that you are switched-on and it's easier to do with less stress.

**STEP 7. WHERE ARE YOU NOW?**

Now that you've completed the Balance for Planning for Sales Calls, it's time to reassess your level of improvement or change from your responses to the questionnaire on page 90. You'll find the questions that relate to this particular Balance below.

Place a check mark in the column on the right that most clearly reflects your level of agreement or disagreement with each statement below. Now, turn to page 90 again to compare your current response with your initial response. Additionally, I urge you to mark your calendar and re-check your responses a month from now to assess your continued improvement. Many people find that their improvement level increases even more a month later.

| | | Strongly Agree | Agree | Doesn't Apply | Disagree | Strongly Disagree |
|---|---|---|---|---|---|---|
| 5. | I research potential clients prior to contacting. | | | | | |
| 6. | I easily and comfortably surf the web. | | | | | |

## STEP 8. IT'S TIME TO CELEBRATE:

If you're Self Muscle Checking or Noticing, congratulate yourself. If you're working with a partner, celebrate the successful completion of the Balance for Planning for Sales Calls and switching yourself on.

## STEP 9. REINFORCING THE BALANCE WITH HOME PLAY:

Each time you finish reading and doing the Balances for the day, there's one more step before you end your Switched-On Selling session. Home play reinforces and enhances the re-wiring and rebalancing in the brain so the Balance will hold. Go to Chapter 14 on page 223 and follow the directions there.

**NOTE:** If you are continuing to work in this current session, skip this step and go on to the next chapter. Then turn to Reinforcing with Home Play after the last Balance.

# CHAPTER 10

# PROSPECTING

**Identifying Your Trigger Points:**

As you read through Tony's strategies in this chapter, you may want to write down any Trigger Points or Hot Button issues on page 163 as you go along. Or, if you prefer, you can read the entire chapter and then write your responses. Either way works just fine. (If necessary, review the instructions on Trigger Points on page 95.)

For many salespeople, finding good prospects is a major step on the road to success. How can you identify those prospects who are most likely to want to hear your message? And once you've identified the profile of those most likely to buy, where can you find prospects who fit your profile in large numbers?

Unless you are just starting in sales, look to your existing customer base for clues. Your current customers can point the way to others who might purchase in the future, because you'll probably find that your existing customers and your best potential prospects have similar demographic and psychographic profiles. By demographics we mean that they have similar incomes, occupations, or educational levels, are in the same industries, have similar structures or distribution systems, hold the same position within the company, etc. By psychographics we mean that they share similar beliefs, attitudes, values, priorities, and buying patterns.

Here's a good example of how you might use demographic profiling of your existing customers to help you find new prospects. Suppose a review of your most profitable accounts shows that you've had success in the past selling your computer system to multi-branch banks. It would make sense to keep calling on multi-branch banks and to place a higher priority on them than you would on hardware stores where you've never sold a system. You might build on that success by calling on organizations that have a similar structure in similar industries, such as multi-branch consumer lending companies.

## Why Do Your Customers Buy?

If you were to ask your current customers specifically why they bought from you and they responded by saying that they felt comfortable with you because of your reputation for 24-hour support, high quality products or services, or your money back guarantee, you would have the beginnings of some psychographic data or, in other words, a profile of their *buying values*. To refine it a little bit more, you might ask them to reduce their reason for buying to one word or one sentence. In this case they might say "reliability and peace of mind." When approaching other prospects, you would then use reliability and peace of mind as your focus for talking about your competitive advantage and point to your reputation for 24-hour support, error-free software, and your one-year money-back guarantee as support for your claim of reliability and peace of mind.

Don't just guess or assume. Look at your demographic and psychographic data. You may be surprised to find out that the customers you regard as major accounts aren't necessarily the volume leaders; high visibility doesn't always translate into high volume. And often you'll find that the high volume accounts aren't necessarily the high profit accounts. They may be discounted deeply or require more servicing than some smaller accounts. Your current best customers may not be your current biggest customers. So how do you identify your best customers? Your study should begin with an analysis of your sales over the last two to three years. If you are new to sales or to your company, look to experienced salespeople or to your sales managers for help here. In your analysis, you'll look for three things:

1. Who bought what?
2. Exactly how did we find and sell those customers?
3. Why did they buy what they bought?

First, you want to look at who bought what. Which customers accounted for your past sales? What products or services did they buy and how much did they buy? Which sales were the most profitable? Which ones had the shortest sales cycle? Take a close look at which industry and segment of the market these accounts are in. The United States Chamber of Commerce has a coding system for every industry group and subgroup as well. They are called SIC codes or Standard Industrial Classifications. Identify which SIC codes your best customers belong to. The reference librarian at your local library can help you. Your goal is to identify the patterns in your high-volume and high-profit customers—the ones who provided the most valuable business to your company.

It's sometimes strategically valuable to sell to a customer who might not be high-profit, but who is high-prestige. Sometimes a company wants an industry leader on its customer list because of its high profile in a given industry. The fact that the leader has selected you can influence others to do business with you as well.

Some companies want to build market share regardless of volume and profit. If your company's primary focus is on building market share, you'll want to target *all* the possible prospects who could buy your product. Whichever factors you use, determine the profile of your company's best customers: Who bought what?

## Customer Source Patterns

Next, look at the sources of your best customers. Exactly how was that business acquired? Where did the initial contact come from? Was it a referral, a cold call, a walk-in, a trade show lead, or was it in response to an ad or a trade journal article you wrote? Who handled it initially, and who finally brought in the business? Look for *patterns!* Find out what you are doing that is working. Success leaves clues, so look for them. This will help you to focus on your highest leverage opportunities for reaching similar prospects. If you can find a pattern in your existing customer profiles you should be able to find new prospects who are likely to buy by finding other companies who fit the pattern of your existing customers. After you've got a good profile of what your best customers look like and you've discovered the patterns that have brought you together successfully in the past, ask yourself where you can find lots more prospects that fit your profile.

Whatever you find out is valuable information because it tells you how you can best represent your products and services to prospective customers, and it will give you some insights into the ways your customers see you, your company, and your products.

By now, you should have a clear picture of what types of buying preferences typify your "best" customers. This, then, allows you to identify prospects who fit that "best customer" profile. Using the criteria set forth in your analysis, you can identify potential buyers who are likely to have the same needs and might buy for the same reasons as your best current accounts.

There's one more common denominator to look for in this analysis when you're selling to the business market. Which contacts in the customers' organizations have you had the most success with? What position within the company do most of your first contacts and ultimate buyers hold? Is it the president, vice president of marketing, director of operations, director of M.I.S., purchasing manager, or someone else? Identifying these key contacts will let you know to whom you should direct your selling efforts.

Every company is different. Sometimes it does make sense to go to the person most likely to buy your product, such as the purchasing department. But more often, it makes more sense to go to the highest-level person in the company who recognizes the problem your product or service solves. In a small company, that might mean calling on the president or CEO. In a larger company, that might mean contacting someone at the executive level, a director or vice president. Keep in mind that in the selling process you'll need to meet the needs of gatekeepers, users, buyers, influencers, and decision-makers, but ultimately it's the decision-maker who needs to say yes. Starting too low in the organization could be the kiss of death. The president or department head may not be the one who places the order with you, but he can provide valuable information on the company, and he can tell you whom you need to see to get action. Besides, what better way to get in to see the purchasing manager than to say the president referred you?

Let's review what we've covered so far. To find those common denominators that make up your "best customer" profile, identify who bought what, exactly how you got those customers, and why they bought what they bought from you. The answers to these three questions will help you target your best potential customers and increase your likelihood of success. It will also help you to start thinking about segments of the market that you may not have thought about before.

So far you've learned how to identify your best current customers and create a profile for the kinds of prospects you want to go after. Next, we'll cover how to use classic prospecting sources to generate a regular supply of qualified leads.

One of the first things you can do is be sure you're doing something in addition to working your current leads or sitting at your desk waiting for the phone to ring. Successful salespeople don't make their money solely off company leads! They develop their own business and social contacts. They ask their friends if they know of any people who might be interested in financial planning or insurance products. They give seminars and lectures to groups of target prospects regarding financial security, estate planning, retirement planning, or funding educational needs for children. They send direct mail to the owners of businesses or target market prospects such as doctors or CPAs. They find out what kinds of business and social activities their profile prospect is likely to engage in, whether it's golf or Chamber of Commerce meetings, and they join and participate. They get involved in civic and professional groups to build a reputation. They know the more visible they are with their prospects, the more likely prospects will do business with them.

Also, investigate former customers who, for some reason are no longer doing business with your company. One reason may simply be that they haven't been called on in a while because the salesperson who originally sold them is no longer with your company. These former accounts represent a gold mine right under your nose.

And remember, prospects are everywhere. Casually talk to the parent sitting next to you at your child's after-school baseball game. A sale could be sitting right next to you!

Do your prospects play golf? Consider joining them for an afternoon round. Always be thinking, "What could I do for this particular prospect that would allow him or her to experience the value of financial planning?" If you make sure it's convenient and easy for them, your prospecting can be much more successful.

Your goal is to make sales. What lies before you, however, is a great deal of research, preparation, and legwork. Look at it this way. Imagine that you're in the plant business. You grow houseplants and carry twelve varieties, each of which blooms in a different month of the year. So you have a different plant available each month of the year. Each of these plants, however, requires twelve months to grow from seedling to full bloom. In addition, each plant requires attention once a month. This attention includes feeding, watering, pruning, and rotation. So you set up a schedule in which you plant the seeds a year in advance and then every month do what is required to continue or start the growth of each plant. The pay-off doesn't come until a year after you've started, but each month thereafter a new plant will be ready to sell. You're all set—unless you forget a step some month. However, you probably won't discover your oversight until many months down the line. By then it will be too late. In the plant business, you can't plant the seeds on the thirteenth of the month and expect to have a sale on the first.

The development of your business as a salesperson also requires investing in a future payoff. The time lag between planting your seeds and reaping the rewards varies. Each month, however, you must do what is necessary to ensure a future yield. The maintenance and growth of your business requires that you: (1) continually replenish your source of prospective clients, (2) qualify prospects to determine their eligibility as clients, (3) study the needs of each prospect, and (4) propose solutions to prospect's needs.

## Sources of Prospects

### Tip Clubs and Business Networking Groups

Tip clubs and business networking groups can be a helpful resource as they are set up for members to share tips and resources with other members. This type of give-and-take results in a group synergism. Each person is able to bring to the group his area of expertise, centers of influence, social networks, and business contacts. With everyone bouncing ideas off one another, a kind of professional kinetic energy develops in which everyone can gain information, cross-sell, obtain referrals, and increase the drive to achieve. Most groups meet on a regular basis over breakfast or lunch. They often have a short program during which a member can describe his or her product or service. Most of these groups follow a few simple guidelines. Check out BNI Clubs Worldwide at www.Ecademy.com and www.LinkedIn.com.

## Canvassing

Canvassing can be a potential source of prospects if you follow some simple guidelines. Before you contact people or firms in your area, they should be qualified. Because they are unsolicited prospects, study their situation to determine any obvious need for your products and services. Determine when seems to be a good time/quiet time to contact them. If done with sincerity, interest, and research, canvassing can expand your prospect reservoir significantly.

## Existing Customers

Satisfied customers represent an excellent source of prospects for you. They'll talk to their friends and associates about their purchases, and they may mention your name. Occasionally a customer will tell you the name of an associate, but this is rare. So it's up to you to probe your customers tactfully for referrals. This is a habit you could cultivate after each sale or call. If you're always tactfully asking customers for referrals, perhaps they'll think of some for you even when you're not there. If nothing else, they'll be impressed with your enthusiasm and "stick-to-it-ivity."

Most professional salespeople say the most effective way to obtain referrals is to ask specific leading questions. One way of doing this is to review your list of qualifying criteria for prospects. Choose one criterion and base your question on it. For example, let's say one of your qualifying criteria is that the prospect is the owner of their own company. You would then ask your client, "Who do you know who wants to reward their key employees or supplement their profit-sharing plan with a minimal effect on current cash flow?" You should then remain silent, giving your customer time to think.

When a customer is giving you referrals, especially if there's more than one, jot them down without analyzing them. After he's finished, you can go back and question him on qualifying details.

Your customers are some of the most valuable resources for referrals that you have. They know other business people in their field and are in the best position to recommend you to them. For this reason, you should ask your client if you could mention his name when contacting someone he referred to you. Through your customers you'll find new branches to follow to tap prospective clients.

## Professional Groups

Consider joining organizations comprised of prospects within your target markets. As an individual, become involved with your family, friends, and different community groups. You'll lead a more fulfilled life if you're active and interested in the world around you. And there's certainly nothing wrong with letting people know what you do and of your willingness to be of service to them. In the natural course of conversation we're always asked, "What do you do?" However, be aware that one of the fastest ways to turn people off is to launch into a sales pitch. Simply tell them what you do and leave it at that. Later, if you see that you may be of some service to them, you can approach them and discuss it in a relaxed and helpful way.

Once you get to know everyone in the organization (if it's small enough for you to do so), you can try to obtain a membership list or directory. You are then in a position to systematically contact each one in an informative, casual way. It's not advisable to send "blanket" direct mailings.

## Directories & Internet Searches

In addition to the *Yellow Pages,* you can find directories on everything imaginable at your local library. These directories can be a gold mine and will save you time and energy. Some list specific people to contact, such as corporate officers or department heads. *The Polk Directory* lists everyone living in every city in the United States, along with their occupation. This puts you in a position to send an introductory letter to as many people as you wish. (See www.CityDirectory.com) There are also directories for specific industries such as the hotel and travel industry. Better yet, with the increasing sophistication of Internet search engines, such as Google, Yahoo, Bing, etc., you can conduct your searches right from your business or home computer, most likely faster and more completely than by using paper-based directories.

## Other Prospects

Many new salespeople assume that if a prospect doesn't buy, there is no potential left in the relationship. Not so. A prospect can be asked for referrals in the same way that established clients are asked. With a prospect, however, it is paramount that you create a professional business relationship before asking for referrals. If you're perceived as being credible, trustworthy, and ethical, your prospect will have no qualms about referring you to others. In fact, the better your relationship with a prospect, the harder he'll work to think of referrals for you. When they can, people like to help those they like.

## Centers of Influence

A center of influence is someone in a position to steer you to prospects or steer prospects to you, such as an accountant, attorney, or banker. Focus on building a trusting relationship with them BEFORE asking for referrals. Be sure they know the benefits you have given other clients. Let them know your goals, so they can be aware of the kind of prospects you're looking for. Make sure they know that you sincerely want their help. Give them a formal presentation describing your services or products. Provide them with an extensive list of testimonials, personal and business references, and a professional resume. Centers of influence are very concerned about referring only those salespeople who will not undermine their reputations. Be sure you report back to the center of influence after you contact the person referred. And finally, find a professional way to reciprocate or to say "thank you."

### Friends and Social Contacts

Friends and social contacts can provide a rich source of prospects. It's not uncommon to learn that your friends and relatives have only a vague idea of what you do. Whether you can sell to them is secondary. Like any prospects, they may be able to refer you to others. Just qualify them before making contact with them or adding them to your social networking groups (such as Twitter, Facebook, Plaxo, LinkedIn, etc.).

After the initial contact, for those you want to continue networking with, devise a method of maintaining contact. Start snail mailing, e-mailing, or maintaining contact through social networking. Be sure to update your online social networking profile periodically. Twitter your thoughts or special messages to keep your contacts up to date on you. Newsletters, brochures, direct mail correspondence, and greeting/special occasion cards all will serve you well. I use a service called Send Out Cards that snail mail's greeting cards with my own personal message (www.SendOutCards.com).

Just keep in mind that when you approach a friend or relative, it's best to do it in a low-keyed manner.

### Chambers of Commerce

The local Chamber of Commerce is also an excellent place to prospect—especially for the small business market. It is their job to keep up to date on local businesses and to aid in their development. For example, if your targeted market was non-profit organizations and charitable giving, the local Chamber would very likely have a listing. The information is relatively easy to get and is usually free.

### Study Groups

Study groups have become a very effective tool for strengthening a salesperson in his or her career. A study group is an in-person or online assemblage of individuals involved in similar activities. They form close, business-related friendships to help each other grow and develop as sales professionals. At each in-person or virtual meeting, they bring one another up to date by comparing notes on recent events, types of strategies planned, obstacles encountered and overcome, and other insights. Each member strengthens the others by offering observations, assessments, feedback, and support. Just make sure the group is kept noncompetitive.

### Trade Associations

If your target market consists of a very specific type of business, there is a good chance that most firms in this business belong to a trade association. The association could be very helpful in providing you with information on its membership. Most trade associations publish a monthly or quarterly magazine for their membership. This could keep you up to date on trends and issues in your target market industry. The trade association might also have for sale a mailing list of its membership. This could be helpful when you are doing your direct mail prospecting.

### Newsletter or EZine

The rate of technical advancement in practically every field is so great that few individuals can keep abreast of it. If you have a thorough understanding of the changes in your field and a knack for writing, you're in a prime position to produce a monthly or quarterly newsletter or ezine in which you call attention to new products, services, and technological improvements. This would provide a service to your clients and prospects and save them time. It would also keep you in their mind as someone with whom to do business.

## The Prospecting Plan

Now let's look at some general ideas to keep in mind when prospecting. First of all, no matter what source of prospecting you utilize, ALWAYS have a prospecting plan. The basic elements include (1) setting objectives, (2) classifying prospects, and (3) evaluating your results.

The objectives set for your prospecting plan should be very similar in nature to any other type of marketing objective you would develop. All objectives should be:

(1) QUANTIFIABLE. This means they must be measurable for purposes of evaluation. Measurement criteria should also be specified, such as identifying and contacting so many new prospects per month.

(2) Objectives should also be REALISTIC, while at the same time motivating you.

(3) They should be TIME SPECIFIC. Without a beginning and an end the objectives will be of little value.

(4) They should be put IN HIERARCHICAL ORDER. If more than one objective is needed, rank them in terms of importance.

Once you've identified prospects you want to contact, classify and record them according to categories that are meaningful to you. For professionals, you could divide them by doctors, lawyers, architects, etc. For centers of influence, there would be accountants, attorneys or bankers. For business prospects, there would be subdivisions for small businesses owners, partnerships, professional corporations, key executives, and so on. In addition to WHOM to talk to, you could target the TYPE of sale such as whole life, disability, annuities, general financial planning, etc.

To assist you with implementing this, create a "Prospect Data Sheet." It should include pertinent data, such as the prospect's name, company name, address, phone, category of account, type of prospect, and a record of the actions you have taken, with dates and the actions you intend to take.

Getting business requires creative prospecting and a comprehensive prospecting plan. If you have a plan, and you work the plan, you'll have an unending flow of qualified prospects and consistently high sales.

---

# BALANCE FOR PROSPECTING

*In this Balance, we will be working on being able to effectively, comfortably, and even enjoyably find new customers and clients.*

## STEP 1. TRIGGER POINTS:

We're now going to give you the opportunity to identify the Trigger Points that came up for you in this chapter and write them down. Does anything that you've just read act as a "Hot Button issue" for you? If you need an explanation of Trigger Points, go to page 95.

| TRIGGER POINTS | POSITIVE GOAL STATEMENTS |
|---|---|
|  |  |
|  |  |
|  |  |
|  |  |
|  |  |

## STEP 2. CALIBRATION: Preparing for the Process

If necessary, refer to the more detailed instructions on Calibration on page 71.

1. **Need for Water:** To make sure you are not dehydrated, drink some water.
2. **Electrical Circuitry:** To make sure your electrical circuitry is operating efficiently, do The Brain Buttons (page 61).
3. **Activating:** To make sure your body is ready to move, do The Cross Crawl (page 65).
4. **Stress Reduction:** To make sure your stress response is deactivated, do Hook-ups (page 63).

5. **Method to Use:** Select whether you will do Muscle Checking with a Partner, Self Muscle Checking, or Noticing (page 54).
6. **"Yes"/"No" Response:** Use the biofeedback response method you chose to ask your body for a "yes" and then a "no" response (page 45).

**NOTE:** When you are in the middle of a Balance, it's possible you may begin to get inaccurate or questionable results. While this rarely occurs, it is a possibility. In case it does occur, simply repeat the Calibration procedure, and then proceed with the Balance, beginning at the point where you began to experience the inaccurate or questionable results.

**STEP 3. CHECKING THE ISSUES: Statements and Actions**
    **A. TRIGGER POINTS:**

If you wrote down any statements from Tony's material, do Muscle Checking with a Partner, Self Muscle Checking, or Noticing on both the negative side and the positive goal side of what you wrote. If you are Muscle Checking with a Partner, read the statements out loud. You should be switched-off for both. If you are not switched-off, then what you thought was a negative Trigger Point is not one.

    **B. ASPECTS OF PROSPECTING:**

Make the following statements one at a time and do Muscle Checking with a Partner, Self Muscle Checking, or Noticing to determine if your body is switched-on or off after saying each statement. These statements are here to make sure all aspects of the Prospecting process are covered and that you are switched-on for the complete process of Prospecting. If you are Muscle Checking with a Partner, read it out loud. Place a check mark next to any statements for which you are is switched-off.

      \_\_\_\_\_ 1. "I feel confident and competent with all my prospects."

_____ 2. "I capably and effectively find cold call leads."

_____ 3. "I enjoy finding cold call leads."

_____ 4. "I make a good first impression with my prospects."

_____ 5. "I easily and effectively approach the real decision makers in an organization."

_____ 6. "I easily, effectively, and enthusiastically make phone calls to prospects."

_____ 7. "I quickly and confidently develop credibility with a prospect on the telephone."

_____ 8. "I quickly and confidently develop credibility with a prospect in person."

_____ 9. "I am effective during face-to-face visits with prospects."

_____10. "I am positive and confident when I am networking with others."

## C. YOUR OWN ISSUES AND CHALLENGES:

Write your own positive affirmations if there are aspects of Prospecting that you still feel are an issue or challenge for you. While you have written those as positive statements, you should be switched-off when you do Muscle Checking with a Partner, Self Muscle Checking, or Noticing. It is okay not have to have any statements that you want to add.

_____11. _____

_____12. _____

_____13. _____

If you were switched-on for all of these statements, it means you don't have any major issues or difficulties with this aspect of the selling process. If this is the case, skip to Step 5 and do the Brain Gym movements and exercises in that step. By doing the Brain Gym movements and exercises, you can increase and improve upon aspects of the sales process that are already positive for you and move yourself to an even higher level of success.

### D. ACTIONS:

Now do a physical action, role play, or visualization for twenty seconds or so for each of the Trigger Points and the Statements you placed a check mark next to in Step 3-B and C for which you were switched-off. Do Muscle Checking with a Partner, Self Muscle Checking, or Noticing for each action as soon as you complete it. Place a check mark next to each action for which you are also switched-off.

## STEP 4. CHOOSING TO INCLUDE THE PAST:

In a moment you will be saying to yourself (or out loud to your partner, if you are working with a partner):

"My system now incorporates, in the most appropriate way, all relevant past events, known and unknown, into the Step 3 experience." (See page 45 for explanation for what a "yes" or "no" mean).

Now do Muscle Checking with a Partner, Self Muscle Checking, or Noticing.

## STEP 5. TAKING ACTION: Doing the Brain Gym Movements

Now's the time for you to do the Brain Gym movements listed below. (See the instructions and illustrations for each of the Brain Gym movements in Chapter 4 beginning on page 59.)

- The Cross Crawl (see page 65)
- The Grounder (see page 67)
- The Calf Pump (see page 65)
- The Footflex (see page 67)
- Belly Breathing (see page 61)
- The Positive Points (see page 69)
- Hook-ups (see page 63)
- Lazy 8s (see page 63)
- Brain Buttons (see page 61)

**STEP 6. CHECKING THE CHANGES: Statements and Actions**

Now you're going to repeat Step 3. This time you should be switched-on for all of the Statements and Actions.

**A. TRIGGER POINTS:**

Say out loud each of the trigger statements that you wrote and do Muscle Checking with a Partner, Self Muscle Checking, or Noticing for each one. You should now be switched-on for all of them.

**B. ASPECTS OF PROSPECTING:**

Say the following statements out loud and then do Muscle Checking with a Partner, Self Muscle Checking, or Noticing. You should now be switched-on for all of them.

1. "I feel confident and competent with all my prospects."
2. "I capably and effectively find cold call leads."
3. "I enjoy finding cold call leads."
4. "I make a good first impression with my prospects."
5. "I easily and effectively approach the real decision makers in an organization."
6. "I easily, effectively, and enthusiastically make phone calls to prospects."
7. "I quickly and confidently develop credibility with a prospect on the telephone."
8. "I quickly and confidently develop credibility with a prospect in person."
9. "I am effective during face-to-face visits with prospects."
10. "I am positive and confident when I am networking with others."

**C. YOUR OWN ISSUES AND CHALLENGES:**

If you wrote any of your own statements down in Step 3-C, read them now. Do Muscle Checking with a Partner, Self Muscle Checking, or Noticing for each one. You should now be switched-on for every one of them.

## D. ACTIONS:

Now you will repeat the actions you were switched-off for in Step 3 above, again doing each of them for twenty seconds or so. This time when you do the action, you will find that you are switched-on and it's easier to do with less stress.

## STEP 7. WHERE ARE YOU NOW?

Now that you've completed the Prospecting Balance, it's time to reassess your level of improvement or change from your responses to the questionnaire you originally filled out on page 90. You'll find the questions that relate to this particular Balance below.

Place a check mark in the column on the right that most clearly reflects your level of agreement or disagreement with each statement below. Now, turn to page 90 again to compare your current response with your initial response. Additionally, I urge you to mark your calendar and re-check your responses a month from now to assess your continued improvement. Many people find that their improvement level increases even further a month later.

|  |  | Strongly Agree | Agree | Doesn't Apply | Disagree | Strongly Disagree |
|---|---|---|---|---|---|---|
| 7. | It is easy for me to make cold calls using the phone. |  |  |  |  |  |
| 8. | It is easy for me to make cold calls in person. |  |  |  |  |  |
| 9. | I am comfortable talking on the phone. |  |  |  |  |  |
| 10. | I am comfortable with face-to-face visits. |  |  |  |  |  |

## STEP 8. IT'S TIME TO CELEBRATE:

If you're Self Muscle Checking or Noticing, congratulate yourself. If you're working with a partner, celebrate the successful completion of the Balance for Prospecting and switching yourself on.

## STEP 9. REINFORCING THE BALANCE WITH HOME PLAY

Each time you finish reading and doing the Balances for the day, there's one more step before you end your Switched-On Selling session. Home play reinforces and enhances the re-wiring and rebalancing in the brain so the Balance will hold. Go to Chapter 14 on page 223 and follow the directions there.

**NOTE:** If you are continuing to work in this current session, skip this step and go on to the next chapter. Then turn to Reinforcing with Home Play after the last Balance.

# CHAPTER 11

# THE PRESENTATION

**Identifying Your Trigger Points:**
As you read through Tony's strategies in this chapter, you may want to write down any Trigger Points or Hot Button issues on page 185 as you go along. Or, if you prefer, you can read the entire chapter and then write your responses. Either way works just fine. (If necessary, review the instructions on Trigger Points on page 95.)

Each prospect has a unique situation that needs to be explored before you can give a solution-oriented presentation. Exploring the prospect's business, needs, and opportunities may require extensive research and repeated trips to his office, factory, or home.

## Need Versus Opportunities

It is important to explore a prospect's situation for problems and opportunities. The only two ways we can help customers with our product or service is if it solves a problem for them or helps them capitalize on a new opportunity.

One important difference between problems (or needs) and opportunities is that needs are the gap between what a customer wants and what he has. This needs/gap problem cannot be created ... either it exists or it doesn't. However, new opportunities can be created, such as potential sources of new markets, avenues of distribution, promotional vehicles, and so on.

For instance, let's assume you are a computer salesperson talking to a prospect in the advertising business and you find out that his business is slow. As you continue to talk with this prospect, he shares his belief that one reason his sales are low is because he's not staying in touch with his clients enough. They don't realize all the things he can do for them. You recognize an opportunity and ask him if he's ever thought of doing a newsletter for his customers. You explain how easy it would be for him to design professional-looking newsletters … using the templates on the desktop publishing software that comes with the computer.

By finding out about your customer's problems and opportunities, you have become a partner to your customer, giving him ideas to help build his business.

Look for opportunities; find niches that your prospect may not have been aware of. Explore your prospect's industry. What are his competitors doing? What trends may be affecting his business now or in the future?

To determine if your product or service will be of any value to your prospect, you must know his current situation, all of its attendant problems, the potential of the business, and his goals and objectives. For example, if your prospect has an unorganized payroll but no desire to be more organized, there is no sense in trying to sell efficiency in the beginning. Note the phrase: "in the beginning." At first, you should accept your prospect's assessment of his situation as valid from his point of view or current personal reality. As you develop trust within the relationship, you will be in a position to bring up new ideas that he might not have previously addressed. When you have a strong relationship, you can mention the unorganized payroll and show him a way to save time and money. Having confidence in your expertise at that point, the prospect will be open to your suggestions in creating a future-focused, growing personal reality for him.

One of the primary reasons for the exploring stage is to give you a picture of the actual conditions surrounding the prospect versus the desired conditions. Often prospects think their goals are being accomplished, when in reality, they are not. They are too close to the situation to see it objectively. After establishing a healthy relationship, it is your responsibility to analyze their situation and point out opportunities they may be missing.

After analyzing a prospect's business, if you find his need gap to be small, then your product or service may offer little or no improvement. In this situation, your advice would be not to buy. When this happens, wrap up the call so you will not waste either your time or the prospect's. You might conclude by saying something like, "Mr. Jones, based on what we've discussed it looks as if I can't offer you a way to improve your sales. If in the next six months, however, you find your sales do not grow by more than 5 percent (or some other condition), we would have a basis for doing business. Do you mind if I keep in touch to see how your sales are progressing?"

When you terminate a call in this manner, your prospect will remain open to future contacts because you did not try to sell him something he did not need. You have planted seeds of good will and trust, which will reap future benefits. Place that prospect's name on a follow-up list and call in six months. When you reach the prospect, ask how things are in general and then ask questions to see if those specific conditions have changed. If they have not changed, ask if you can call back again in six months. If they have changed, get together and review the situation again. At this point, you will already have established trust—a huge asset—and you will be able to pick up from where you left off.

In the majority of cases, after analyzing your prospect's need gap, you will often find that you can be of service.

## Exploration Tool: Smart Questions

The purpose of exploring is to get information: an accurate picture of the customer's needs and what it will take to provide an effective solution. To do so, we need to listen to what the customer says, but we also need to know how to ask the right questions to get the information we need.

Asking intelligent questions is a critical sales skill. It does not require asking many questions—just the right ones. The art of questioning is the cornerstone of exploring the customer's needs. It is paramount to a successful career in sales. Asking questions is similar to painting a picture. We start with a blank canvas and begin to fill in the background and rough in the picture with broad-brush strokes. Then we fill in the details using finer and finer strokes.

With questioning, we start with broad strokes asking the customer broad, open questions that rough in a lot of his situation. "Tell me about your business" not only starts to give you information about your prospect's situation, it gives him a chance to relax and tell you what he thinks is important. If you start with a smaller brush, "What was your sales level last year?" you may miss an important opportunity because sales may not be what your prospect's primary concern right now.

Broad, open-ended questions show your interest in the prospect's situation. They often start with "Tell me ...," "How," "What," "Why."

- "How do you see a computer system fitting into your situation?"
- "What would you like a computer to do for you?"
- "Why are you looking at computer systems right now?"

These open-ended questions are much more powerful than closed-ended questions that require a simple yes or no answer or a specific piece of information.

Questions should move at a pace that is comfortable for the prospect. He may be hesitant to provide information that is either sensitive or threatening. An inexperienced salesperson who is convinced that his product or service is right for the customer may leap to the question of budget (before the customer decides he or she wants to spend anything at all), thereby risking the possibility of killing the sale prematurely.

There will be many times when you may have to ask a sensitive question. When the need arises, be sure to tell the customer the reason for your question. For example, while opening a new savings account, the new accounts officer may ask, "What's your mother's maiden name?" That may sound personal or odd and put you on the defensive. However, if it were explained that this is for your protection, and that their tellers will ask for your mother's maiden name anytime someone tries to cash a check for over $500 against your account, then you would feel more comfortable sharing such sensitive information.

Questions are the basis of your information gathering activities but it is also important to understand the three primary directions for questions. They are:

1) **Expand:** When you want more information or background data about a certain area, ask an expansion question. You are trying to get a broader picture: "Tell me more about that …" "How would that work?" "What would that mean to you?"

   For example, a woman sees an ad, and calls a landscaper to quote the design and installation of a rock garden. After arriving and establishing rapport (connecting), the landscaper asks "expanding" questions. The landscaper gets her to describe her vision for a perfect rock garden. "How would it look from your window?" "How prominent would the garden be in relation to the rest of the property?" "What types of things would be in your rock garden?" She begins opening up and sharing her dreams to the landscaper.

2) **Clarify:** These are questions we ask when we need more details or when we need to verify a perspective or point-of-view. We are focusing in on a single issue: "I'm not quite sure I understand …" "Can you give me an example?" "Do you mean …"

   Returning to our example…

   By asking some "clarifying" questions, the landscaper discovers that she speaks about flowers more often than rocks. By refocusing his questions on flowers, he learns that she is an avid nature photographer. She immediately pulls down a photo album containing pictures she has taken; revealing him shot after shot of … butterflies! What she *really* wants is photo opportunities … and flowers that attract butterflies would be ideal!

3) **Redirect:** When you want to build on a person's position or change directions, you acknowledge the current issue and then ask question that brings up a new issue. "Okay I think I understand what you think (feel) you need here; what if you could also have ..."

In our example, the landscaper might respond with, "If I've heard you correctly, you would love a garden that attracts exotic butterflies. I happen to have written a published article about horticulture's role in landscape design. If you like, I will call my secretary and have her send you a copy ... my gift to you. The article contains a section focused on flowers that produce pollen; the nectar that attracts butterflies. By the way, how might someone's knowledge about flowers influence your decision in hiring your landscape designer?"

What a great "redirecting" question! You can see how close he is to landing a new client ... the mutual bond is forming.

"Direction" questions (expand, clarify, and redirect) help us steer through the exploring process. A skillful salesperson uses this stage to guide the prospect to tell him what he needs to know to provide an appropriate, effective solution.

## Features Versus Benefits

New salespeople are often confused by the difference between features and benefits and the role each plays in a presentation. A feature is an aspect of the product or service that exists regardless of the customer's need for it. A benefit is the use or advantage a customer derives from a feature. For example, a customer who is shopping for a truck may not care about four-wheel drive. It is a feature, but an irrelevant one to some people. However, when an off-road enthusiast walks up to the truck, that feature suddenly becomes a benefit.

A benefit, then, is a feature in action. Most customers, especially end-users on the retail level, think in terms of benefits. They don't care what features make something work. They are only concerned with the end result—the benefits they can derive from the purchase.

During a presentation, you must know what kind of person you are dealing with. If you are selling to an engineer, you must discuss features as well as benefits. Most of the time, however, you will not need to cover features in such detail. In fact, most final decision-makers only care about the bottom line, which is how they will benefit from the purchase.

Concentrate on speaking the language of benefits. This means addressing your prospect's problems or needs one at a time and showing how your product/service will solve each specific problem. Get your prospect involved by using the Feature-Feedback-Benefit (FFB) method. Present a feature and ask for feedback. For example:

Salesperson: "This computer has a 500 gig hard disk. How important is that to you?"

Customer: "I don't know. Is that enough to store at least 2,000,000 names for a mailing list?"

The customer has done two things:

1) Revealed a lack of knowledge and need for consultative help; and

2) Described an important benefit that must be provided by the product. Later in your presentation, you would come back to this benefit and make a point of showing how it will be provided.

Keep in mind that a feature can provide more than one benefit. Similarly, a described benefit can be accomplished with more than one feature. For example, a fireplace can provide more than heat. The benefit of recreation can be derived from a swimming pool, a big backyard, a finished basement, or proximity to a park.

During your presentation, be sure to point out all the possibilities, especially if flexibility and diversity are desired benefits. In addition, use the following questions, or similar ones, to uncover other desired benefits:

- "How do you see this fitting into your current or future situation?"
- "Have I missed any advantages that this may provide you? What might they be?"
- "This is how my product/service can be used in 'Situation A'; can you see ways that it will help you with 'Situation B'?"
- "How do you see this addressing the problem/opportunity we discussed earlier?" (Be specific)
- "Does this look like it will meet your needs?"

If the answer is no, say, "I'm sorry, I must have missed something. What are you looking to accomplish that I have overlooked?"

## Proposing Solutions

If your prospect requires a standard sales presentation, you should:

1. Address each of the prospect's needs one by one, presenting solutions as you go.
2. Cover all issues, but don't discuss every feature, only the relevant ones.

   *Remember:*

   - A **feature** is any aspect of a product or service that exists whether or not it's ever used and regardless of a prospect's needs.
   - An **advantage** is how a feature can be used to help solve a prospect's problem.
   - A **benefit** is a way a specific feature satisfies a specific prospect's need—a benefit is a feature in action. It answers the question, "What's in it for me?"
   - Any single feature can have more than one benefit; any desired benefit can be achieved by more than one feature.

3. Focus on those features that highlight your competitive advantages.
4. Follow a natural or logical order of discussion, or the prospect's priorities.
5. Involve the prospect by using the *feature/feedback/benefit* method: Present the feature, invite feedback, and let the prospect provide the benefit.

Example of the feature/feedback/benefit method:

**SALESPERSON:** *The house has a small, kidney-shaped pool with a Jacuzzi at one end.* (Feature) *How important is that to you and your family?* (Feedback)

**PROSPECT:** *I have a bad back. I've always wanted a Jacuzzi, and my kids love to swim. A pool and a Jacuzzi would be great!* (Benefit)

Effective feedback questions to ask prospects include:

- How do you see this fitting into your situation?
- What other advantages do you see?
- This is how it fits into your business. How does it fit into your family life?
- How well does this address the opportunities we discussed earlier?
- How well does this look like it will meet your needs?

6. When interrupted, briefly review only the last point you made and continue the presentation. If interruptions are constant, gently address the issue with the prospect, putting the blame on the environment. Offer an alternative environment. As a last resort, offer to reschedule the appointment.

7. Conclude with a benefit summary where you review all the key benefits you'll be providing to the prospect and relate each to his or her specific success criteria.

## Selling Against the Competition

Companies who don't understand their competitive advantage say things like "Our product is better quality" or "Our service is better." Even if a company has better quality or better service, it won't convince customers just by saying so, because many of its competitors will be saying the exact same thing! You have to define quality or show how your service differs from the competition.

The best way to determine your competitive advantage is to break down the components of your product or service into four distinct categories:

**Competitive uniqueness:** What can I do for my customers that no one else can do? What can I offer that no one else can offer?

**Competitive advantage:** What can I do for my customer that my competitor can also do, but I can do it better and I can prove it?

**Competitive parity:** Objectively speaking, my competitors and I are the same here—no real differentiation.

**Competitive disadvantages:** Where does the competition have an advantage over me?

You may want to do your analysis by market segment, by competitor, by product, or all of them, but knowing your competitive position will quickly get you onto your customers' wavelength.

An example of **competitive uniqueness** exists if a pharmaceutical company receives FDA approval to sell a new drug. Since no one else has the drug, this company now has a competitive uniqueness with this drug.

An example of a **competitive advantage** might be where two companies market the same drug, but one is a large, well-known company with wide name recognition and the other is a small, relatively unknown company. If no real competitive advantage exists in your product, try to focus on your company reputation, your excellent service, your responsiveness and reliability, or any other factors than can positively differentiate you from your competition.

In looking at **competitive parity,** review what things are the same between the competition and your product or service but are still important to the customer? Birth control pills are a good example. Several ethical drug companies make different formulations, but all have similar records for preventing pregnancy.

And finally, **competitive disadvantage**—what does the competition do better than you do? Your drug may have more side effects than the competitor's.

By doing this analysis, you'll be in a position to help your customers distinguish between you and your competition.

In order to discover your competitive advantage, you may have to do some intelligence gathering—talk to your customers, your salespeople, watch the local newspapers, attend trade shows, talk to your customers' suppliers, build a file of your competitors' marketing and product information, do a debriefing when you lose a customer to a competitor, use a clipping service to gather information on competitors or on major prospects, obtain annual and quarterly reports of your competitors and prospective customers, watch the market trends in your industry and in your customers' industries—become the expert on your product or service and how it can help your customers.

Knowing and being able to articulate your competitive advantages sets you apart from your competition and clearly shows your customers what your company can do for them that no one else can do.

## Price Concerns

When you get price objections, consider these suggestions:

1. *Clarify what the prospect means when she says your price is too high.*
   - She may mean she can't afford the price, even though she believes the product is worth what you're asking.
     **Strategy:**
     a) Focus on payment options rather than price.
     b) Try creative financing.
     c) Switch to a more affordable product, if available.
   - She may be trying to tell you that her current understanding of the product's features/benefits isn't worth what you're asking.
     **Strategy:**
     a) Review special features and upgrades that make product worth the price.
     b) Check benefits by asking for feedback.
   - She may mean that from her point of view, the product doesn't offer as much as someone else's.
     **Strategy:**
     a) Make sure comparative factors the prospect is using are of equal weight.
     b) Focus on important distinctions and advantages.
   - She may mean that she feels that her money would be better spent on something else (see *Priority* below).
   - She may be trying to tell you that the product is a good value, but not to her, for X reason(s).

**Strategy:**
Create new selection criteria and come up with a new option.

2. *Differentiate between price and total cost.*
   - Price is what you initially pay—a one-time charge.
   - Total cost is what you pay over the term of ownership, including recurring expenses.

3. *Ask the prospect for help in solving the problem. Say something like:*
   - "I sense that you have a concern about money. In an ideal world, how could we structure the financial package to best meet your needs?"

## Postponement Concerns

The first step in dealing with postponement is to uncover the prospect's actual motive.

Postponement is usually expressed as "I want to think it over." The prospect's actual motives can be:

- **A need to go over facts and gather more information.** Show her how she can solve her problems by moving away from what she doesn't want.
- **A need to consult with others.** Encourage her to involve others throughout the process. You may need to go back and "start over" with others who will be involved in the decision.

**Ask these feedback questions to uncover unstated prospect concerns:**
- On which parts of the report are you not clear?
- Which options are confusing?
- Are you still working against a deadline?
- What can I do to help?
- Do you currently have a source for the funds, or will you be looking for one?

When the prospect is unsure of what the problem is, usually she is concerned about the risk involved. Find out how the prospect perceives the risk of your solution. Have her list the pros and cons as she sees them.

**Reduce the prospect's perception of risk by:**
- Offering a money-back guarantee.
- Showing the prospect a successful implementation or setting up a conversation with a satisfied customer.
- Offering a pilot. A pilot is a test of one stage of the project to see if the solution can be implemented successfully. The prospect commits to the entire project, but the pilot allows for adjustments or cancellation after the initial phase has been completed. Ask your prospect to place the entire order up front and pay for it to cement their commitment.

**For Those Who Need to Shop:**
- Educate the prospect on how to shop. (Identify key criteria, questions to ask, and so on.)
- Offer to help. (Provide information on the competition that highlights your company's competitive advantages; provide names of major competitors.)
- Volunteer to serve as a consultant, answering questions that arise during the shopping process.
- Ask for a commitment to discuss the prospect's findings and help compare/evaluate the competitive information gathered (before a decision is made).
- If the prospect is uncertain that your option meets her needs, explore the key issues again (expected outcome, budget, timing, decision process, and so on).
- Offer a tentative confirmation to the prospect who likes your solution but wants to check out what else is out there. The prospect commits to buy but reserves the right to cancel under specified conditions.

# Product Concerns

There are situations when trust is strong and resistance is due to product problems beyond your control. For example, you may be expected to provide a color or style of an item that is no longer available. Unless the color or style can be changed, the sale may not be confirmed. These problems are difficult but not insurmountable. Help your prospect clearly see her priorities with this four-step process:

1. **Listen** and carefully **observe** both the verbal and the nonverbal message of the prospect. What is really being said?
2. **Clarify** the basis of the resistance so that there is no misunderstanding about what concern you are addressing.
3. **Answer** the concern, using the compensation technique.
4. **Confirm** the prospect's acceptance of your answer to assure that your response was on target and additional resistance is no longer necessary to guide you further.

Using the **Compensation Method,** you acknowledge a deficiency in a particular area of your product or service but try to compensate for it by pointing out other features and benefits that outweigh the shortcoming. For example, if you cannot meet a delivery date, suggest other times and stress the advantages of another date. This method is effective when the shortcoming is not of paramount importance. Suggested alternatives will often suffice.

Sometimes you can use the classic Ben Franklin Balance Sheet. Take a sheet of paper and divide it into two columns with "Reasons For" at the top of the left column and "Reasons Against" at the top of the right column. On this balance sheet, start with the "Reasons For" column and ask your prospect to list all of the reasons why she should make a positive decision to purchase your product. Together rank them from most important to least important.

Next, go on to the "Reasons Against" column and do the same thing. Rank and discuss each of the items on the "Reasons Against" side. Answer the questions your prospect poses and offer a solution or explanation if one exists. You can then ask your prospect if this item is still a negative or if it is now a neutral. It is the *prospect's choice* to delete it from the list or leave it, but at least you have shed some light on the issue. At the end of this process, ask your prospect how she would like to proceed.

# Balance for Making Presentations

This Balance is designed to optimize your ability to make presentations to clients and potential clients, including the opening, establishing rapport, handling objections, asking for the order, and preventing feelings of rejection.

## The Balance for Making Presentations is divided into Section I and Section II

The Statements and Actions in Section I focus on the macro aspects of making a presentation, which include listening and communicating. Section II contains the micro elements, which make up all the elements in your ability to present. It is presented in these two sections because I want to make sure you are switched-on at all levels of presenting.

# SECTION I - The Major Elements

### STEP 1. TRIGGER POINTS:

We're now going to give you the opportunity to identify the Trigger Points that came up for you in this chapter and write them down. Does anything that you've just read act as a "Hot Button issue" for you? If you need an explanation of Trigger Points, go to page 95.

| TRIGGER POINTS | POSITIVE GOAL STATEMENTS |
|---|---|
|  |  |
|  |  |

| TRIGGER POINTS | POSITIVE GOAL STATEMENTS |
|---|---|
|  |  |
|  |  |
|  |  |

**STEP 2. CALIBRATION: Preparing for the Process**

If necessary, refer to the more detailed instructions on Calibration on page 71.

1. **Need for Water:** To make sure you are not dehydrated, drink some water.

2. **Electrical Circuitry:** To make sure your electrical circuitry is operating efficiently, do The Brain Buttons (page 61).

3. **Activating:** To make sure your body is ready to move, do The Cross Crawl (page 65).

4. **Stress Reduction:** To make sure your stress response is deactivated, do Hook-ups (page 63).

5. **Method to Use:** Select whether you will do Muscle Checking with a Partner, Self Muscle Checking, or Noticing (page 54).

6. **"Yes"/"No" Response:** Use the biofeedback response method you chose to ask your body for a "yes" and then a "no" response (page 45).

**NOTE:** When you are in the middle of a Balance, it's possible you may begin to get inaccurate or questionable results. While this rarely occurs, it is a possibility. In case it does occur, simply repeat the Calibration procedure, and then proceed with the Balance, beginning at the point where you began to experience the inaccurate or questionable results.

**STEP 3. CHECKING THE ISSUES: Statements and Actions**
    **A. TRIGGER POINTS:**

If you wrote down any statements from Tony's material, do Muscle Checking with a Partner, Self Muscle Checking, or Noticing on both the negative side and the positive goal side of what you wrote. If you are Muscle Checking with a Partner, read the statements out loud. You should be switched-off for both. If you are not switched-off, then what you thought was a negative Trigger Point is not one.

    **B. ASPECT OF MAKING PRESENTATIONS:**

Make the following statement and do Muscle Checking with a Partner, Self Muscle Checking, or Noticing to determine if your body is switched-on or off. This statement is here to make sure this aspect of making presentations is covered and that you are switched-on for it. If you are Muscle Checking with a Partner, read it out loud. Place a check mark next to the statement if you are switched-off.

\_\_\_\_\_ "I listen and communicate effectively with clients."

    **C. YOUR OWN ISSUES AND CHALLENGES:**

Write your own positive affirmations if there are aspects of making presentations that you still feel are an issue or challenge for you. While you have written those as positive statements, you should be switched-off when you do Muscle Checking with a Partner, Self Muscle Checking, or Noticing. It is okay not have to have any statements that you want to add.

\_\_\_\_\_ 1. _____
\_\_\_\_\_ 2. _____
\_\_\_\_\_ 3._____

If you were switched-on for all of these statements, it means you don't have any major issues or difficulties with this aspect of the selling process. If this is the case, skip to Step 5 and do the Brain Gym movements and exercises in that step. By doing the Brain Gym movements and exercises, you can increase and improve upon aspects of the sales process that are already positive for you and move yourself to an even higher level of success.

### D. ACTIONS:

Now do a physical action, role play, or visualization for twenty seconds or so for each of the Trigger Points and the Statements you placed a check mark next to in Step 3-B and C for which you were switched-off. Do Muscle Checking with a Partner, Self Muscle Checking, or Noticing for each action as soon as you complete it. Place a check mark next to each action for which you are also switched-off.

### STEP 4. CHOOSING TO INCLUDE THE PAST:

In a moment you will be saying to yourself (or out loud to your partner, if you are working with a partner):

"My system now incorporates, in the most appropriate way, all relevant past events, known and unknown, into the Step 3 experience." (See page 45 for explanation of what a "yes" or "no" means).

Now do Muscle Checking with a Partner, Self Muscle Checking, or Noticing.

### STEP 5. TAKING ACTION: Doing the Brain Gym Movements

Now is the time to do the Brain Gym Movements listed below:

- The Cross Crawl (see page 65)
- Lazy 8s (see page 63)
- Brain Buttons (see page 61)
- The Elephant (see page 66)
- The Thinking Cap (see page 69)
- The Owl (see page 68)
- The Footflex (see page 67)
- The Positive Points (see page 69)
- Hook-ups (see page 63)

**STEP 6. CHECKING THE CHANGES: Statements and Actions**

Now you're going to repeat Step 3. This time you should be switched-on for all of the Statements and Actions.

**A. TRIGGER POINTS:**

Say out loud each of the TRIGGER STATEMENTS that you wrote and do Muscle Checking with a Partner, Self Muscle Checking, or Noticing for each one. You should now be switched-on for all of them.

**B. ASPECT OF GOAL SETTING:**

Say the following statement out loud and then do Muscle Checking with a Partner, Self Muscle Checking, or Noticing. You should now be switched-on for it. "I listen and communicate effectively with clients."

**C. YOUR OWN ISSUES AND CHALLENGES:**

If you wrote any of your own statements in Step 3-C, read them now. Do Muscle Checking with a Partner, Self Muscle Checking, or Noticing for each one. You should now be switched-on for every one of them.

If you had no Trigger Points and were switched-on for all of the Statements in 3B and 3C, that means you don't have any major issues with this aspect of the selling process. If this is the case, skip to Step 5 and do the Brain Gym movements and exercises to move yourself to an even higher level of success.

**D. ACTION:**

Now do a physical action, role play, or visualization for any of the statements above for which you were switched-off, again doing each of them for twenty seconds or so. Do Muscle Checking with a Partner, Self Muscle Checking, or Noticing for all the actions that relate to statements you were switched-off for in Step 3-A and B. Put a check mark on the line below if you were switched-off for it:

_____ For thirty seconds, role play giving your sales presentation to a client. (If you are working by yourself, imagine that you are making a sales presentation to a prospect. Do Muscle Checking with a Partner, Self Muscle Checking, or Noticing.

# SECTION II - The Sub-Elements

Now that you have completed Section I, you are switched-on for your overall aim of being able to communicate and listen during the presentation process. In Section II of this Balance, I have broken down the components of the presentation for you to look at all of the sub-elements of presenting so you can be sure you are switched-on for them as well. For example, while you may be good at listening and communicating, when it comes to answering objections or asking for the order you might still be switched-off.

If you are switched-on for all of the presentation statements in Step 7 below, you can simply go to Step 11 to finish the Balance. However, if there are any statements that you are switched-off for, continue through the rest of the Balance until all of the Statements and Actions are switched-on.

### STEP 7. CHECKING THE SUB-ELEMENTS: Statements and Actions
### A. ASPECTS OF PRESENTATIONS:

Make the following statements and do Muscle Checking with a Partner, Self Muscle Checking, or Noticing to determine if your body is switched-on or off for each one. Place a check mark next to any statements for which your body is switched-off.

_____ 1. "I am comfortable and effective when I start a sales call."

_____ 2. "I establish rapport quickly and easily with my client."

_____ 3. "I listen to my client's needs and desires."

_____ 4. "I know my product or service well and understand its uses and applications."

_____ 5. "I ask effective and appropriate questions."

_____ 6. "I easily and successfully answer objections."

_____ 7. "I am confident about asking for the order."

_____ 8. "I successfully handle feelings of rejection."

_____ 9. "I secure the sale and prevent buyer remorse."

## B. YOUR OWN STATEMENT:

Write your own positive affirmations if there are aspects of making presentations that you still feel are an issue or challenge for you. While you have written those as positive statements, you should be switched-off when you do Muscle Checking with a Partner, Self Muscle Checking, or Noticing. It is okay not have to have any statements that you want to add.

_____ 10. _____

_____ 11. _____

_____ 12. _____

## C. ACTION:

Now do a physical action, role play, or visualization for twenty seconds or so for each of the statements you were switched-off in Step 7-A and B. Do Muscle Checking with a Partner, Self Muscle Checking, or Noticing for each action as soon as you complete it. Place a check mark next to each action for which you are also switched-off.

_____ 1. Opening

_____ 2. Rapport

_____ 3. Listening

_____ 4. Product Knowledge

_____ 5. Probing

_____ 6. Handling Objections

_____ 7. Closing

_____ 8. Handling Rejection

_____ 9. Securing the Sale

_____ 10-12. Your Own Statements

## STEP 8. CHOOSING TO INCLUDE THE PAST:

In a moment you will be saying to yourself (or out loud to your partner, if you are working with a partner):

"My system now incorporates, in the most appropriate way, all relevant past events, known and unknown, into the Step 3 experience." (See page 45 for explanation for what a "yes" or "no" mean).

Now do Muscle Checking with a Partner, Self Muscle Checking, or Noticing.

## STEP 9. TAKING ACTION: Doing the Brain Gym Movements

Now is the time to do the Brain Gym Movements listed below:

- The Cross Crawl (see page 65)
- Lazy 8s (see page 63)
- Brain Buttons (see page 61)
- The Elephant (see page 66)
- The Thinking Cap (see page 69)
- The Owl (see page 68)
- The Footflex (see page 67)
- The Positive Points (see page 69)
- Hook-ups (see page 63)

## STEP 10. CHECKING THE CHANGES: Statements and Actions
### A. ASPECTS OF MAKING PRESENTATIONS:

Say the following statements out loud and then do Muscle Checking with a Partner, Self Muscle Checking, or Noticing and you should be switched-on for all the statements.

1. "I am comfortable and effective when I start a sales call."
2. "I establish rapport quickly and easily with my client."
3. "I listen to my client's needs and desires."
4. "I know my product or service well and understand its uses and applications."

5. "I ask effective and appropriate questions."
6. "I easily and successfully answer objections."
7. "I am confident about asking for the order."
8. "I successfully handle feelings of rejection."
9. "I secure the sale and prevent buyer remorse."

## B. YOUR OWN ISSUES AND CHALLENGES:

If you wrote any of your own statements in Step 7-C, read them now. Do Muscle Checking with a Partner, Self Muscle Checking, or Noticing for each one. You should now be switched-on for every one of them.

## C. ACTIONS:

Now you will repeat the actions you were switched-off for in Step 3 above, again doing each of them for twenty seconds or so. This time when you do the action, you will find that you are switched-on and it's easier to do with less stress.

## STEP 11. WHERE ARE YOU NOW?

Now that you've completed Section I and II of the Balance for Making Presentations, it's time to reassess your level of improvement or change from your responses to the questionnaire you originally filled out on page 90. You'll find the questions that relate to this particular Balance below.

Place a check mark in the column on the right that most clearly reflects your level of agreement or disagreement with each statement below. Now, turn to page 90 again to compare your current response with your initial response. Additionally, I urge you to mark your calendar and re-check your responses a month from now to assess your continued improvement. Many people find that their improvement level increases even further a month later.

| | | Strongly Agree | Agree | Doesn't Apply | Disagree | Strongly Disagree |
|---|---|---|---|---|---|---|
| 11. | I effectively begin the presentation. | | | | | |
| 12. | I develop a rapport quickly with a client. | | | | | |
| 13. | I effectively answer objections and questions. | | | | | |
| 14. | I am comfortable asking for the order and closing the sale. | | | | | |
| 15. | I handle rejection well. | | | | | |

## STEP 12. IT'S TIME TO CELEBRATE

If you're Self Muscle Checking or Noticing, congratulate yourself. If you're working with a partner, celebrate the successful completion of Section I and II of the Balance for Making Presentations and switching yourself on.

## STEP 13. REINFORCING THE BALANCE WITH HOME PLAY

Each time you finish reading and doing the Balances for the day, there's one more step before you end your Switched-On Selling session. Home play reinforces and enhances the re-wiring and rebalancing in the brain so the Balance will hold. Go to Chapter 14 on page 223 and follow the directions there.

NOTE: If you are continuing to work in this current session, skip this step and go on to the next chapter. Then turn to Reinforcing with Home Play after the last Balance.

# CHAPTER 12

# FOLLOW-UP: ASSURING CUSTOMER SATISFACTION

**Identifying Your Trigger Points:**

As you read through Tony's strategies in this chapter, you may want to write down any Trigger Points or Hot Button issues on page 203 as you go along. Or, if you prefer, you can read the entire chapter and then write your responses. Either way works just fine. (If necessary, review the instructions on Trigger Points on page 95.)

The attitude of the sales professional is summed up in the following statement by one of the nineteenth century's most successful entrepreneurs, Marshall Field, who founded the Marshall Field Department Stores:

> *"Those who enter to buy, support me. Those who come to flatter, please me. Those who complain, teach me how I may please others so that more will come. Only those hurt me who are displeased but do not complain. They refuse me permission to correct my errors and thus improve my service."*

Field's sales philosophy establishes the customer as the person to whom you are responsible. Customers support you; therefore, they deserve VIP treatment. When your customers are happy, you are happy. When they complain, you are unhappy, but you examine the complaint calmly and see it as an opportunity to learn as well as satisfy their needs. The quote echoes the fear that customers will not vocalize their dissatisfaction, but instead take their business elsewhere.

There's another quote that's even more important to salespeople and companies immediately upon making a sale: "The Sale Begins When the Customer Says ... **Yes**." In the old days, it used to be: "The Sale Begins When the Customer Says ... **NO**," but that's a totally inappropriate attitude to embrace in today's customer-driven business environment. Depending on whether you get a yes or no, you need to either follow up or follow through with each and every prospect/customer.

What is your "follow-up reputation" in your business? Is it "always and promptly"? Or, is it "usually fairly timely"? Or, could it be "doubtful it will get done"? The highest performers keep their promises and exceed the expectations of their prospects and clients. Be a bear about this one. It isn't a task to be dreaded; it is an opportunity to be seized. You can set yourself apart with good follow-up skills. What is the difference between "following up" and "following through"?

If your prospect declines or delays the decision to do business with you, you still have obligations to that person, which requires *following up*. If they do become your customer, you need to follow through; ensuring that every promise is completely fulfilled.

Let's take a look at the bad news first: No sale! Now it's time to do some follow up with this prospect.

First, the prospect deserves to be sincerely thanked for her time and for giving you an opportunity to exchange information. A hand-written note is always appreciated and sets you apart from a vast majority of salespeople that take shortcuts.

Next, you need to stop and objectively reflect upon the circumstances that caused the prospect to say, "No, thank you." Depending upon the situation, you may have a high likelihood of landing the account sometime down the road.

Here is a list of questions that you should ask yourself when debriefing each sales call:

- Did they decline because I proposed a solution before *fully* exploring their needs and collaborating solutions with them?
- Did I do my best possible job of asking questions and encouraging them to share their ideas, or did I do too much "presenting" of my ideas and possible solutions?

- Did I adjust to their *pace* (faster versus slower) and to their *priority* (task versus relationship)?
- Am I confident that I helped them make the best possible decision that is in <u>their</u> best interests?
- By behaving respectfully and professionally, have I left the door open for doing business later if their situation changes?
- Based on their reasoning for not buying, might the situation change in the future?

True sales masters become comfortable hearing "no" as long as they have *gotten to the real reason(s) for the answer.*

After careful, objective analysis, you are now fully prepared to follow up with this prospect. We believe that in many cases you can often turn a "no" into a "yes" if you execute *customized, long-term follow-up campaigns.*

It is common for salespeople to be in the right place (a qualified prospect), but at the wrong time. Many prospects, if empowered to educate themselves over time, can—and often do—change their own minds. However, no one likes to have to do so in front of a salesperson.

There are two different types of follow-ups that you can execute; each serves a specific function.

The first is a standard type of follow-up. The salesperson sends literature, case studies, testimonials, and other "value proposition" information designed to further educate the prospect about the value your product/service delivers. Sometimes this does work, but no matter how cleverly disguised, it might convey a message similar to: "You didn't say 'yes' during our discussion, so here's evidence that may help you change your mind."

While this "traditional" practice of marketing is acceptable, it can be improved. Although educating prospects is never a bad idea, "attention erosion" is making it harder to get your messages received, read, and digested. Businesspeople today are over-taxed, stretched thin, and have little time to spare reading your literature and newsletters.

However, we bring good news: The second type of follow-up makes the first type much more effective …

Dale Carnegie taught us that to get what you want, first help others get what they want. He said that if we live our lives helping others achieve their goals, everything we desire will come back ten-fold. We heartily agree.

"Treat others the way *they* want to be treated," is our mantra. It's The Platinum Rule®. By blending the Carnegie philosophy with ours, then adding a mix of cutting-edge technology, we were able to create a new method of following up with everyone in a customized, effective manner that ensures marketing messages are received with open arms (and open minds!).

*Goal-specific Communication* is the act of sending people (prospects, customers, clients, colleagues, referral partners, etc...) information that *helps each of them achieve specific goals or seize a new opportunity.*

If you take the time to ask interesting questions and pay careful attention to answers, you can now leverage technology to automate follow-ups that send articles, tips, and ideas to each of your contacts that match their goals, challenges, interests, and preferences.

**Pay careful attention to this statement:** If you send people helpful information—*especially if it is <u>unrelated</u> to what you sell*—you will position yourself as a helpful, thoughtful professional, and not as a pesky, pushy salesperson.

**Here's an example:** Let's say that Scott Zimmerman (Tony's partner in The Platinum Rule Group) is calling on a sales manager and exploring ways to possibly help the sales team develop new skills and create more effective marketing messages. While Scott's company happens to provide solutions in these areas, he also discovers that the prospect is relatively new to his position and has not received formalized management training. Additionally, he learns that they invest large amounts of time, focus, and money attending several trade shows.

After the sales call, Scott executes a "blend" of follow-ups for this prospect. Using Scott's patented Cyrano Marketing System, he selects a series of articles written by experts in the areas of interviewing, hiring, managing, and interpersonal communications, all containing information that the prospect would find helpful in becoming more successful in his career. These are "relationship building" messages which are chosen specifically to help this prospect become a more effective manager. These messages contain no information about Scott, his company or his products; they *only* serve to help the prospect.

When the prospect receives a few emails or articles from Scott, he begins to perceive Scott as someone who is thoughtful, and also as someone who takes action on his ideas. As you might imagine, this type of communication begins building a bridge between Scott and each prospect.

When Scott calls back, he immediately offers to introduce the prospect to one of his colleagues who happens to be an expert in trade show marketing and long-cycle lead conversion. Couple that with the helpful articles on management skills that Scott emails, and Scott has earned the respect of his prospect by adding value at each touch point of the relationship.

More importantly, this approach dramatically increases the odds that when Scott sends "value proposition" information (literature, case studies, etc.) that the prospect will receive each message with an open mind.

By truly helping each prospect, Scott has *earned* "mind share" with each person. By matching messages to the goals, preferences, and interests of every prospect, Scott eliminates "attention erosion." People in Scott's Cyrano database actually anticipate his follow-up messages!

If Scott discovers that the timing is poor with a prospect, he "fills the time" by sending helpful information to him. If the prospect suggests that Scott call back in six months or so, he tells Cyrano what type of articles to send, when he wants them sent, and asks for Cyrano to remind him to call back at the appropriate time. In other words, Scott doesn't get frustrated when he is in the right place at the wrong time. Instead, he simply leverages this to his advantage. He fills the time gaps by showing the prospect that he cares about their success. This ensures that when Scott calls back, his phone calls are eagerly accepted and/or his voicemails get prompt return calls.

As many thought leaders often remind us: *If you want to get everything you want, first help others get what they want!*

While conducting our sales training programs, we are often asked if adapting to different styles and/or sending helpful information may be "manipulative."

Our stock answer is, "It depends." If you do it right it is not. If you handle it with a win-lose approach it certainly can be.

If your ***intention*** is to help other people; help them make decisions that are in the best interest of their company and/or career (even if it means not buying your product or service), help them achieve more, help them solve problems and help them succeed, then you are in no way practicing any form of manipulation. You are living The Platinum Rule. You are leveraging the power of persuasion in a positive fashion to create win/win outcomes in your business relationships.

However, if your intention is simply to make a sale, mislead another person, or do anything that is even one percent less than ethical, then we can confidently state that you ***are*** using adaptability, technology, and persuasion in a manipulative fashion.

As Malcolm Gladwell pointed out in his best-selling book *Blink*, almost every person has the innate ability to detect authenticity in another person in mere seconds. As importantly, they do it on a subconscious level; *without even knowing they are doing so.*

If your intention is pure, prospects and clients will subconsciously be compelled to want to do business with you. Conversely if your intention is to make money, push people into making buying decisions, and/or manipulation, then no amount of training, psychology, or technology will help you build a long-lasting career in sales.

Here are some important questions you should pose to your sales manager and to your marketing manager:

- Are we effectively leveraging information gleaned from the field (sales calls)?
- Is our contact management system (or CRM) being used to full capacity?
- Are we effectively communicating with everyone in our database?
- Does every one of our prospects know about each product and/ or service that we offer and why they should be buying from us?
- Are we effectively cross-selling to each customer who makes a purchase with our company?
- Should we consider matching our benefits to behavioral styles of our prospects?

- Since it is now possible to automate customized follow-ups (even if salespeople forget), would we grow our sales if we added effective technology to our process?
- Do we have a *system* for developing leads, cross-selling, increasing customer retention, and growing referrals?

These are very important questions for your team to consider.

While it is important for you to learn how to adapt to each prospect or customer during your sales process, it is equally as important for you to market/communicate effectively to ensure that you have a steady stream of qualified prospects, your current customers feel appreciated and thought of often, and you never lose another client due to perceived indifference. You must keep your customers happy.

## Handling Customer Complaints

Whether your customer's complaint is legitimate or not, follow it up with a service call. Whenever possible, do it personally instead of sending someone from the customer service department. It provides the personal service that your customer appreciates, and it may prevent the need for a technician or serviceman to call. As an alternative, both of you can go together to handle customer complaints. Keep the following guidelines in mind:

1. Don't procrastinate in making the call. Often the problem is not as serious as it sounds. Some customers "read the riot act" when they call about a complaint. A delay in responding will only irritate your client more.

2. Admit mistakes and apologize. Just because you made the sale does not mean you should become defensive about your company, product, or service. Even the most reputable companies make mistakes and have problems with their products. You may want to restate the customer's complaint to show that you are listening and have an understanding of the problem.

3. Show compassion for your customer. Whether the complaint proves to be true or false, show your customer that you are concerned and will investigate the problem immediately. Help the customer calm down by saying "I can understand why you feel the way you do."

4. Actively listen to your customer's complaint. Talking will make him feel less anxious about it. Let your customer "vent" his feelings before you react to the situation. Be sympathetic and encourage the customer to "blow up." Afterward, he'll feel better; this means he'll be in a better frame of mind.

5. Don't pass the buck to your company or someone else within it. This may take the blame off you, but it undermines the integrity and organization of the company, and your customer will lose confidence in your firm.

## Maintaining Customer Satisfaction

The philosophy behind maintaining your customers is simple; now that you have them, maintain them. When you consider the amount of time and money invested in them, you cannot afford to lose them. This investment goes beyond your personal expenditures. It also includes your firm's advertising and marketing costs to reach that particular market segment. Your customers, therefore, should be treated as if the life of your business depended on them—which it does!

The bottom line in maintaining your clients is service, service, and more service. Be there for your customers and they'll want to stick with you. If you meet their needs, they'll think twice before switching to another company, even if they've voiced some serious concerns. "Make new clients, but keep the old. One is silver and the other gold." Develop the "gold" you have, and the silver may take care of itself.

# BALANCE FOR FOLLOW-UP

The Balance for Follow-Up is designed to help you achieve the best possible on-going relationship with your clients, including aspects such as writing proposals, offering up-sells, customer service, and asking clients for referrals.

## STEP 1. TRIGGER POINTS:

We're now going to give you the opportunity to identify the Trigger Points that came up for you in this chapter and write them down. Does anything that you've just read act as a "Hot Button issue" for you? If you need an explanation of Trigger Points, go to page 95.

| TRIGGER POINTS | POSITIVE GOAL STATEMENTS |
|---|---|
|  |  |
|  |  |
|  |  |
|  |  |
|  |  |

## STEP 2. CALIBRATION: Preparing for the Process

If necessary, refer to the more detailed instructions on Calibration on page 71.

1. **Need for Water:** To make sure you are not dehydrated, drink some water.
2. **Electrical Circuitry:** To make sure your electrical circuitry is operating efficiently, do The Brain Buttons (page 61).
3. **Activating:** To make sure your body is ready to move, do The Cross Crawl (page 65).
4. **Stress Reduction:** To make sure your stress response is deactivated, do Hook-ups (page 63).
5. **Method to Use:** Select whether you will do Muscle Checking with a Partner, Self Muscle Checking, or Noticing (page 54).
6. **"Yes"/"No" Response:** Use the biofeedback response method you chose to ask your body for a "yes" and then a "no" response (page 45).

**NOTE:** When you are in the middle of a Balance, it's possible you may begin to get inaccurate or questionable results. While this rarely occurs, it is a possibility. In case it does occur, simply repeat the Calibration procedure, and then proceed with the Balance, beginning at the point where you began to experience the inaccurate or questionable results.

## STEP 3. CHECKING THE ISSUES: Statements and Actions

### A. TRIGGER POINTS:

If you wrote down any statements from Tony's material, do Muscle Checking with a Partner, Self Muscle Checking, or Noticing on both the negative side and the positive goal side of what you wrote. If you are Muscle Checking with a Partner, read the statements out loud. You should be switched-off for both. If you are not, then what you thought was a Trigger Point is not one.

### B. ASPECTS OF FOLLOW-UP:

Make the following statements one at a time and do Muscle Checking with a Partner, Self Muscle Checking, or

Noticing to determine if your body is switched-on or off after saying each statement. These statements are here to make sure all aspects of the follow-up process are covered and that you are switched-on for the complete process of following up with prospects. If you are Muscle Checking with a Partner, read it out loud. Place a check mark next to any statements for which you are is switched-off.

____ 1. "I easily and effectively write proposals."

____ 2. "I offer other opportunities to my clients."

____ 3. "I am attentive to the needs of my customers."

____ 4. "I ask my customers for referrals."

____ 5. "I easily, effectively, and in a timely way complete all paperwork."

C. **YOUR OWN STATEMENTS:** Write your own positive affirmations if there are aspects of Follow Up that you still are an issue or challenge for you. After you have written those statements, you should be switched-off when you do Muscle Checking with a Partner, Self Muscle Checking, or Noticing. It is okay not have to have any statements that you want to add.

____ 6. _____

____ 7. _____

____ 8. _____

____ 9. _____

If you had no Trigger Points and were switched-on for all of the Statements in 3B and 3C, that means you don't have any major issues with this aspect of the selling process. If this is the case, skip to Step 5 and do the Brain Gym movements and exercises to move yourself to an even higher level of success.

D. **ACTIONS:**

Now do a physical action, role play or visualization for twenty seconds or so for each of the Trigger Points and Aspects of Follow-Up that you placed a check mark next to in Step 3-B and C for which you were switched-off. Do

Muscle Checking with a Partner, Self Muscle Checking, or Noticing for each action as soon as you complete it. Place a check mark next to each action for which you are also switched-off.

**STEP 4. CHOOSING TO INCLUDE THE PAST:**

In a moment you will be saying to yourself (or out loud to your partner, if you are working with a partner):

"My system now incorporates, in the most appropriate way, all relevant past events, known and unknown, into the Step 3 experience." (See page 45 for explanation for what a "yes" or "no" mean).

Now do Muscle Checking with a Partner, Self Muscle Checking, or Noticing.

**STEP 5. TAKING ACTION: Doing the Brain Gym Movements**

Now's the time for you to do the Brain Gym movements listed below. (See the instructions and illustrations for each of the Brain Gym movements in Chapter 4 beginning on page 59.)

- The Cross Crawl (see page 65)
- Lazy 8s (see page 63)
- Brain Buttons (see page 61)
- Earth Buttons (see page 62)
- Space Buttons (see page 64)
- Balance Buttons (see page 60)
- The Thinking Cap (see page 69)
- The Owl (see page 68)
- The Footflex (see page 67)

**STEP 6. CHECKING THE CHANGES: Statements and Actions**

Now you're going to repeat Step 3. This time you should be switched-on for all of the Statements and Actions.

**A. TRIGGER POINTS:**

Say out loud each of the trigger statements that you wrote and do Muscle Checking with a Partner, Self Muscle Checking, or Noticing for each one. You should now be switched-on for all of them.

**B. ASPECTS OF FOLLOW-UP:**

Say the following statements out loud and then do Muscle Checking with a Partner, Self Muscle Checking, or Noticing. You should now be switched-on for all of them.

1. "I feel confident and competent with all my prospects."
2. "I easily and effectively write proposals."
3. "I offer other opportunities to my clients."
4. "I am attentive to the needs of my customers."
5. "I ask my customers for referrals."
6. "I easily, effectively, and in a timely way complete all paperwork."

**C. YOUR OWN ISSUES AND CHALLENGES:**

If you wrote any of your own statements in Step 3-C, read them now. Do Muscle Checking with a Partner, Self Muscle Checking, or Noticing for each one. You should now be switched-on for every one of them.

**D. ACTIONS:**

Now you will repeat the actions you were switched-off for in Step 3 above, again doing each of them for twenty seconds or so. This time when you do the action, you will find that you are switched-on and it's easier to do, with less stress.

**STEP 7. WHERE ARE YOU NOW?**

Now that you've completed the Balance for Follow-up, it's time to reassess your level of improvement or change from your responses to the questionnaire on page 90. You'll find the questions that relate to this particular Balance below.

Place a check mark in the column on the right that most clearly reflects your level of agreement or disagreement with each statement below. Now, turn to page 90 again to compare your current response with your initial response. Additionally, I urge you to mark your calendar and re-check your responses a month from now to assess your continued improvement. Many people find that their improvement level increases even more a month later.

| | | Strongly Agree | Agree | Doesn't Apply | Disagree | Strongly Disagree |
|---|---|---|---|---|---|---|
| 16. | I offer my clients other opportunities. | | | | | |
| 17. | It is easy for me to ask my clients for referrals. | | | | | |
| 18. | It is easy for me to write proposals. | | | | | |
| 19. | I provide effective customer service. | | | | | |
| 20. | I easily and effectively complete all paperwork. | | | | | |

## STEP 8: IT'S TIME TO CELEBRATE

If you're Self Muscle Checking or Noticing, congratulate yourself. If you're working with a partner, celebrate the successful completion of the Balance for Follow-Up and switching yourself on.

## STEP 9: REINFORCING THE BALANCE WITH HOME PLAY

Each time you finish reading and doing the Balances for the day, there's one more step before you end your Switched-On Selling session. Home play reinforces and enhances the re-wiring and rebalancing in the brain so the Balance will hold. Go to Chapter 14 on page 223 and follow the directions there.

**NOTE:** If you are continuing to work in this current session, skip this step and go on to the next chapter. Then turn to Reinforcing with Home Play after the last Balance.

# CHAPTER 13

# BEING A PROSPEROUS SALESPERSON

**Identifying Your Trigger Points:**

As you read through Tony's strategies in this chapter, you may want to write down any Trigger Points or Hot Button issues on page 214 as you go along. Or, if you prefer, you can read the entire chapter and then write your responses. Either way works just fine. (If necessary, review the instructions on Trigger Points on page 95.)

Prosperity can take many forms for a salesperson—higher income, more sales, happier customers, more personal self-fulfillment, etc. Let's cover some items that can really improve your happiness, success, and prosperity.

## Happiness is a Way of Traveling, Not a Destination

The only advantage of being a pessimist is that all your surprises are pleasant. But that's pretty small change compared to the big payoff that comes from projecting positive expectations.

Much of our happiness or unhappiness is caused, of course, not by what happens, but how we look at what happens. In other words, by our thinking habits. And habits can be changed.

In his book, *Power Talking*, George Walther shows how you can foster the mind-set that interprets setbacks as positive opportunities. He believes this is a skill that you can develop—one word, one phrase, and one sentence at a time.

For starters, purge the words "I failed" from your vocabulary, Walther urges. Replace them with "I learned" to help your mind focus on the lessons involved.

Similarly, you might want to get in the habit of a few more vocabulary changes:

- Use the word *challenge* when others would say *problem*
- *I'll be glad to* instead of *I'll have to*
- *I'm getting better at ...* rather than *I'm no good at ...*

The subliminal effect of changing even a few words, Walther says, can prompt your mind to come up with creative solutions rather than dreading or fleeing the problem.

## Failure is the Line of Least Persistence

There likely will be setbacks and occasional self-doubts on the road to maximizing your sales prosperity. You're going to need patience and persistence. But it's important to keep moving toward your goal.

I'm reminded of a friend who had a life-changing experience in a cross-country ski race in Minnesota. He had moved there not long before. In an enthusiastic, if not realistic, effort to adapt to the local culture, he bought some skis, practiced a bit, and entered an advanced competition. He took off like a flash at the sound of the starter's gun. But after the first quarter mile in near-zero temperatures, he knew he was in over his head, hopelessly outclassed by other competitors swiftly gliding past him. He was soon alone in a frozen wilderness, and his thoughts turned gloomily to fatigue and defeat.

He had initially hoped to finish in a couple of hours. But as the cold seared his lungs and the exertion weakened his arms and legs, he all but gave up on his goal. If there had been a way to surrender, he would have. But being in deep snow in the middle of the woods, his only way out was to ski out. So he pushed aside the pain and pessimism, and kept skiing.

He imagined a lodge with a roaring fire that might be just around the bend—but wasn't. He imagined a rescue vehicle slicing through the drifts to pick him up—which didn't. He even imagined a helicopter dropping down to whisk him away—but, of course, that never materialized.

So on and on he skied until, at last, he came to a sign: "FINISH LINE, 1/2 MILE." He couldn't believe it! Energized, he sprinted that last quarter mile and finished in a time not far from his original goal.

My friend often repeats that story, the winds more frigid and his muscles more aching with each retelling. It's become a part of his self-identity, and the memory of his endurance and ultimate triumph has gotten him through other of life's difficult scrapes and struggles. The moral, as he sees it, is that if you keep slogging ahead, refuse to give up, and stay as positive as you possibly can, you'll accomplish your goal, or something very close to it.

I could hardly argue with that. So, even if you have trouble imagining success, keep moving along that snowy path in the woods. And before you know it, you'll have success beyond your imaginings.

## Even the Best Excuse Doesn't Feel as Good as Success

The world, according to author, salesman, and speaker extraordinaire Don Hutson, consists of winners and whiners. "Have you noticed that you seldom hear highly successful people whining?" he asks. Instead, everyone silently cheers when whiners leave the room and take with them their own personal dark clouds with them.

Whiners make excuses; winners just get the job done. In weight-reduction classes, participants are often reminded that being thin feels better than, say, chocolate tastes. That's true for accomplishment, too. Having a good excuse for a poor performance doesn't compare with the thrill of having produced excellent results.

## Don't Become a Stress Victim

I refer to people who work hard but never get the results they want in life as stress victims. Most stress victims work so hard and so long because they get bogged down in too many trivial tasks. Very often the really important jobs, the ones with a high payoff, never get done. This lack of task perspective is very often the direct result of not having clearly defined goals in writing.

By knowing what is truly important in your life and by having clearly written goals and action plans, you are better able to differentiate the high-payoff tasks from the low-payoff tasks. Then, if you spend most or all of your time doing your high priority tasks, you'll probably accomplish twice as much in half the time.

### Learn to Say "No!"

Stress victims have a difficult time telling people they are not able to do another task. They feel it shatters their omnipotent image. Ironically, taking on too much puts so much pressure on the stress victims that the overall quality of their work decreases and their Superman image suffers anyway. When you feel you have more than enough to keep you busy, politely refuse to take on more.

### Learn to Delegate

One of the major problems afflicting stress victims is their inability and unwillingness to delegate tasks to others. They must resist the tendency to do things themselves. Train others, especially your secretary or assistant, to do your routine and low-priority tasks. Also, delegate the right to make mistakes. That's how others learn. Give them their space to do things on their own. You should be spending your time on planning and completing your high-priority tasks.

### Exercise

One of the most effective ways to relieve tension and stress is through exercise. It not only helps you avoid a stress episode, it also helps you circumvent many other physical ailments. Workaholics and super-achievers complain that they do not have the time to exercise. On the contrary, taking time out of a busy schedule to exercise usually makes you feel less fatigued while you're working and actually increases your level of awareness and productivity on the job. Force yourself to get at least three hours of physical activity per week spread out over at least five separate days.

### Break Your Routines

Don't follow too rigid a schedule. Too much structure gets you into a rut. In the field of nutrition, the experts recommend rotational dieting. That simply means not eating the same foods all the time and adding variety and flexibility to your eating habits. The same advice holds true for your daily and weekly work schedule. Purposely go out of your way to do some things differently, to do some new things, and to do them at different times.

## Do Your Best to Relax

Kick back every so often during each day. Let your mind wander, not thinking about anything in particular, and especially not about business. These are necessary recharge breaks. Take long, hot baths at home to relieve tension. You will find that this is an ideal way to relax both your mind and body.

## Eat Lunch Away from the Office

This is an excellent way to accomplish many of the above suggestions. Walking to and from the restaurant or the park is an excellent source of exercise. Eating lunch outside or in the park is an ideal way to relax and cleanse your mind. Leaving the office for meals breaks the routine of being in the office all day.

## Spend More Time with Your Family

I realize that not everyone is married or has a family. Those that do should schedule their family members into their appointment book and respect the entry as they would any other business appointment. Eat at least one meal per day with your family. Try to keep business calls to a minimum at your home. Spend one evening and one-half day per week doing something with your family as a group. (TV watching doesn't count!) Get to really know the people who are very important to you in your life.

## Take Time for Yourself

Get away by yourself intermittently. Spend some time alone getting to know yourself. Meditate. Relax. Read light, enjoyable material. Pursue a hobby that has absolutely nothing to do with your line of work, but is relaxing and enjoyable. Treat yourself—you deserve it.

## Don't Take Life Too Seriously

Believe it or not, you're not indispensable. Not to the world. Not to your country. Not even to your company. Everything will go on with or without you. Let up on yourself and others. Yes, you do make a contribution—maybe even a major one. But don't overestimate your own value and worth. Do what you do and do it well. But, don't kill yourself in the process, because then you're of no value to the people and causes for which you were working. Take care of yourself and enjoy all aspects of your life—not just work. Everyone will be the better for it, especially you.

---

# BALANCE FOR BEING A PROSPEROUS SALESPERSON

**In this Balance, you will be re-educating your brain to release any blockages to creating the prosperity and financial success you want in your sales career.**

**STEP 1. TRIGGER POINTS:**
We're now going to give you the opportunity to identify the Trigger Points that came up for you in this chapter and write them down. Does anything that you've just read act as a "Hot Button issue" for you? If you need an explanation of Trigger Points, go to page 95.

| TRIGGER POINTS | POSITIVE GOAL STATEMENTS |
|---|---|
|  |  |
|  |  |
|  |  |

| TRIGGER POINTS | POSITIVE GOAL STATEMENTS |
|---|---|
|  |  |
|  |  |

**STEP 2. CALIBRATION: Preparing for the Process**

If necessary, refer to the more detailed instructions on Calibration on page 71.

1. **Need for Water:** To make sure you are not dehydrated, drink some water.

2. **Electrical Circuitry:** To make sure your electrical circuitry is operating efficiently, do The Brain Buttons (page 61).

3. **Activating:** To make sure your body is ready to move, do The Cross Crawl (page 65).

4. **Stress Reduction:** To make sure your stress response is deactivated, do Hook-ups (page 63).

5. **Method to Use:** Select whether you will do Muscle Checking with a Partner, Self Muscle Checking, or Noticing (page 54).

6. **"Yes"/"No" Response:** Use the biofeedback response method you chose to ask your body for a "yes" and then a "no" response (page 45).

**NOTE:** When you are in the middle of a Balance, it's possible you may begin to get inaccurate or questionable results. While this rarely occurs, it is a possibility. In case it does occur, simply repeat the Calibration procedure, and then proceed with the Balance, beginning at the point where you began to experience the inaccurate or questionable results.

**STEP 3. CHECKING THE ISSUES: Statements and Actions**
    **A. TRIGGER POINTS:**

If you wrote down any statements from Tony's material, do Muscle Checking with a Partner, Self Muscle Checking, or Noticing on both the negative side and the positive goal side of what you wrote. If you are Muscle Checking with a Partner, read the statements out loud. You should be switched-off for both. If you are not switched-off, then what you thought was a negative Trigger Point is not one.

    **B. ASPECTS OF PROSPERITY:**

Make the following statement and do Muscle Checking with a Partner, Self Muscle Checking, or Noticing to determine if your body is switched-on or off after saying the statement. If you are Muscle Checking with a Partner, read it out loud. Place a check mark next to the statement if you are is switched-off.

       \_\_\_\_ 1.  "I connect with the Source of my abundance and generate abundance in my whole being."

    **C. YOUR OWN ISSUES AND CHALLENGES:**

Write your own positive affirmations if there are still aspects of accepting prosperity that you still feel are an issue or challenge for you. While you have written those as positive statements, you should be switched-off when you do Muscle Checking with a Partner, Self Muscle Checking, or Noticing. It is okay not have to have any statements that you want to add.

      \_\_\_\_ 2. _____

      \_\_\_\_ 3. _____

If you had no Trigger Points and were switched-on for all of the Statements in 3B and 3C, that means you don't have any major issues with this aspect of the selling process. If this is the case, skip to Step 5 and do the Brain Gym movements and exercises to move yourself to an even higher level of success.

## D. ACTIONS:

Now do a physical action, role play, or visualization for twenty seconds or so for each of the Trigger Points or any Statements you placed a check mark next to in Step 3-B and C for which you were switched-off. Do Muscle Checking with a Partner, Self Muscle Checking, or Noticing for each action as soon as you complete it. In addition, place a check mark next to each action below for which you are switched-off.

_____ 1. Write the word "SCARCITY" on a piece of paper, crumple it up, and throw it away. Then do Muscle Checking with a Partner, Self Muscle Checking, or Noticing.

_____ 2. Take out a $20 bill, hold it, and visualize it multiplying. Then do Muscle Checking with a Partner, Self Muscle Checking, or Noticing.

_____ 3. Imagine that another person is handing you money and that you are accepting it. (If you are working with a partner, he should actually hand you money and you should accept it.) Then do Muscle Checking with a Partner, Self Muscle Checking, or Noticing.

## STEP 4. CHOOSING TO INCLUDE THE PAST:

In a moment you will be saying to yourself (or out loud to your partner, if you are working with a partner):

"My system now incorporates, in the most appropriate way, all relevant past events, known and unknown, into the Step 3 experience." (See page 45 for explanation for what a "yes or "no" mean.)

Now do Muscle Checking with a Partner, Self Muscle Checking, or Noticing.

## STEP 5. TAKING ACTION: Doing the Brain Gym Movements
Do the Brain Gym Movements listed below:
- The Cross Crawl (see page 65)
- Lazy 8s (see page 63)
- Brain Buttons (see page 61)
- The Thinking Cap (see page 69)
- Hook-ups (see page 63)
- The Positive Points (see page 69)

## STEP 6. CHECKING THE CHANGES: Statements and Actions
Now you're going to repeat Step 3. This time you should be switched-on for all of the Statements and Actions.

**A. TRIGGER POINTS:**
Say out loud each of the TRIGGER STATEMENTS that you wrote and do Muscle Checking with a Partner, Self Muscle Checking, or Noticing for each one. You should now be switched-on for all of them.

**B. ASPECTS OF PROSPERITY:**
Say the following statement out loud and then do Muscle Checking with a Partner, Self Muscle Checking, or Noticing. You should now be switched-on for this statement.

"I connect with the Source of my abundance and generate abundance in my whole being."

**C. YOUR OWN ISSUES AND CHALLENGES:**
If you wrote any of your own statements in Step 3-C, read them now. Do Muscle Checking with a Partner, Self Muscle Checking, or Noticing for each one. You should now be switched-on for every one of them.

**D. ACTIONS:**
Now you will repeat the Actions you were switched-off for in Step 3 above, again doing each of them for twenty seconds or so. This time when you do the action, you will find that you are switched-on and it's easier to do with less stress.

## STEP 7. WHERE ARE YOU NOW?

Now that you've completed the Balance for Being a Prosperous Salesperson, it's time to reassess your level of improvement or change from your responses to the questionnaire on page 90. You'll find the questions that relate to this particular Balance below.

Place a check mark in the column on the right that most clearly reflects your level of agreement or disagreement with each statement below. Now, turn to page 90 again to compare your current response with your initial response. Additionally, I urge you to mark your calendar and re-check your responses a month from now to assess your continued improvement. Many people find that their improvement level increases even more a month later.

|  |  | Strongly Agree | Agree | Doesn't Apply | Disagree | Strongly Disagree |
|---|---|---|---|---|---|---|
| 21. | I view myself as prosperous. |  |  |  |  |  |

## STEP 8. IT'S TIME TO CELEBRATE

If you're Self Muscle Checking or Noticing, congratulate yourself. If you're working with a partner, celebrate the successful completion of the Balance for Being a Prosperous Salesperson and switching yourself on.

## STEP 9. REINFORCING THE BALANCE WITH HOME PLAY

Each time you finish reading and doing the Balances for the day, there's one more step before you end your Switched-On Selling session. Home play reinforces and enhances the re-wiring and rebalancing in the brain so the Balance will hold. Go to Chapter 14 on page 223 and follow the directions there.

**NOTE:** If you are continuing to work in this current session, skip this step and go on to the next chapter. Then turn to Reinforcing with Home Play after the last Balance.

# PART III

## REINFORCEMENT

BY JERRY V. TEPLITZ, J.D., PH.D.

# CHAPTER 14

# REINFORCING WITH HOME PLAY

Home Play is a series of Brain Gym movements that will reinforce and enhance the re-wiring and balancing that you did in the Balances. As we covered earlier, when you do the Balances, you are creating new neural pathways among the various parts of the brain, including the left and right hemispheres and the corpus callosum, which is the connective tissue in the center of the brain that connects the two hemispheres. You might think of it this way: It's as if you are creating a new highway where previously none existed. When you add the reinforcement, you are turning the highway into a superhighway. That further strengthens and enhances the new pathways that have been created.

First, you will determine if the body needs to do Home Play. If your body indicates that it doesn't need to do any Home Play, that's fine. If that's the case, you'll get a "no" response in Step 2 below and then you'll stop this process. This means you did all the re-wiring and balancing that needed to be done. It's as if you baked a cake and iced it and got to eat it, too!

If you get a "yes" response, you will determine which of the Brain Gym Movements your body wants to do to fully reinforce and integrate the Brain Gym Balances in Switched-On Selling at a deeper level. Then you will ask the body how many times a day and for how many days it wants to do the movements and exercises that it has chosen as reinforcement.

# BRAIN GYM HOME PLAY
# SELECTION PROCESS

**STEP 1. CHECKER SAYS:**

If you are Muscle Checking with a Partner, read the following statement to your partner and muscle check. If you are Noticing or Self Muscle Checking, read it out loud to yourself and check: "This system wants to do the Brain Gym movements and exercises to reinforce the Balances in the Switched-On Selling Seminar." Do Muscle Checking with a Partner, Self Muscle Checking, or Noticing.

If you get a "yes" response, go on to Step 3. If you get a "no," stop. This means your body doesn't need to do any reinforcement. It means your body feels the learning in the Balances is complete.

**Step 2.   CHECKER CONFIRMATION:**

If "yes," say out loud to yourself (or to your partner, if you are working with a partner): "This body wants to do the following movements."

Then read the list of Brain Gym movements listed below. Do Muscle Checking with a Partner, Self Muscle Checking, or Noticing after saying each movement name, then record the names of those you get a "yes" response to on the blank lines below the list. You are not actually going to be doing the movements and exercises right now; you are just creating your reinforcement list.

| | | |
|---|---|---|
| Alphabet 8s | The Cross Crawl | The Calf Pump |
| Arm Activation | Double Doodle | The Elephant |
| Balance Buttons | Earth Buttons | The Grounder |
| Belly Breathing | Hook-ups | The Owl |
| Brain Buttons | Lazy 8s | The Positive Points |
| Calf Pump | Space Buttons | Thinking Cap |

Your List:

_____        _____

_____        _____

_____        _____

_____        _____

_____        _____

_____        _____

_____        _____

_____        _____

## STEP 3. CHECKER CONFIRMATION: Number of Days

Say out loud to yourself (or to your partner, if you are working with a partner):

"This body wants to do these movements at least once a day... at least twice a day... at least three times a day... at least four times a day..." etc.

Do Muscle Checking with a Partner, Self Muscle Checking, or Noticing for each one.

If you get a "yes" response on once a day, check again to see if you should do the movements twice a day. Continue checking until you get a "no" response. For example, if you get a "no" when you check three times a day, that means your last "yes" was two times a day, so you will do the movements twice a day.

## STEP 4. CHECKER CONFIRMATION: Number of Weeks

"This body wants to do these movements for at least one week ... at least two weeks ... at least three weeks ..." etc.

Do Muscle Checking with a Partner, Self Muscle Checking or Noticing for each one.

Let's say you get a "yes" response on one week. Next, you'll check if you should do them for two weeks. Continue checking until you get a "no" response. For example, if you get a "no" response when you check three times a week, this means your last "yes" was two weeks, so you will do the movements for two weeks.

**SUMMARY:** At the end of this process, you will have selected a specific group of Brain Gym movements to do for a certain number of repetitions per day, for a specific number of weeks. Now enjoy your reinforcement.

# CHAPTER 15

# THE SEVEN-MINUTE TUNE UP: REINFORCING BRAIN GYM ON AN EVERYDAY BASIS

The purpose of the Seven-Minute Tune Up is to begin every day on a positive note. It's a way to bring focus, concentration, balance, and energy to your brain and your body. I suggest doing the Seven-Minute Tune Up the first thing every day. You can also do it during the day if something negative happens or if you need to re-energize or refocus during your selling day.

1. **WATER**
   Drink a glass of water.

2. **BREATHE FOR RELAXATION**
   Inhale through the nose while touching the tip of the tongue to the roof of the mouth just behind the teeth. Then drop the tongue and exhale through the mouth. Do this for four to six complete breaths. As an alternative, you can do the Belly Breathing on page 61.

3. **BRAIN BUTTONS**
   Place one hand on your belly button. With the thumb and fingers of the other hand locate the two hollow areas below the collarbone. The hollows are one or two inches away from the sternum, which is the bone that runs down the center of the chest. Rub these areas vigorously for thirty seconds.

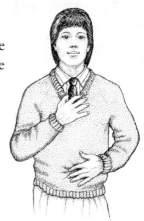

## 4. HOOK-UPS

This movement is done in two parts:

*PART I*

Sit in a chair or stand, clasp your hands together. Whichever thumb is on top will be considered your primary side. Release your hands and extend your hands in front of you with the back of each hand facing the other. Cross the primary side hand over the top of the other hand, intertwine your fingers. Draw your hands under and into your chest.

Cross your primary side ankle in front of the other ankle. Place your tongue against the roof of your mouth, one quarter inch behind your front teeth. Keep breathing through your nose. Hold for thirty seconds.

*PART II*

Uncross your legs. Place the fingertips of both of your hands together, forming a teepee. Keep your eyes closed, the tongue up, and continue to breathe. Hold for thirty seconds.

## 5. THE POSITIVE POINTS

Just above the center of the eyebrows, and halfway up to the hairline you will find a slight bump where the head curves. Place three fingers together lightly on the bumps. Close your eyes and breathe.

Hold the points for thirty seconds to one minute.

## 6. THE CROSS CRAWL

To do The Cross Crawl "march in place,"
lifting the knees high. At the same time, reach
across and touch the knees—or somewhere
on the leg—with the opposite hands.
Continue for thirty seconds.

### *Variations of The Cross Crawl:*

There are other ways to achieve the effect of
The Cross Crawl. You might want to experience
each of them. This will vary the way you do
The Cross Crawl:

- Instead of touching your hands to the
  opposite legs, go all the way down and
  touch the heels. Continue by alternating
  touching opposite hands to the heels.
- Use your elbows instead of your hands to
  touch the knees. Continue by alternating touching
  opposite elbows to the knees. This variation of The Cross
  Crawl stretches the core stomach muscles.
- Touch your left heel behind you with your
  right hand, being sure to keep the left
  hand to the front. Continue by
  alternating touching opposite hands
  and heels to the back.

# APPENDIX A

# CALIBRATION PROCEDURE –
# COMPREHENSIVE METHOD

In Chapter 5 you learned a fast, easy method of Calibration, the process that is used at the beginning of any Balance. As an option, those who are more experienced in the use of Muscle Checking as a biofeedback response system may choose to do this more comprehensive method of Calibration. To do this method you will need to work with a partner.

**PART 1. NEUTRAL:**

> With your partner, do Muscle Checking with a Partner for Normal response, which you learned in Chapter 3 (see page 43). It's important to do this step so you get the feel for your partner's level of resistance. It's also an opportunity for the Checkee to give you feedback so you can determine if the pressure is too hard for his arm.

**PART 2. NEED FOR WATER:**

> The second part of Calibration is to determine if the body is hydrated or dehydrated. In this comprehensive method of Calibration, the procedure used to check if the body is adequately hydrated is an adaptation of a method used by veterinarians to check for dehydration in animals. Vets check the elasticity of the animal's skin by grabbing hold of the skin on the back of the neck, which is called the scruff, and pulling gently or pinching it together and then releasing it. If the animal's body has enough water, the skin quickly springs back to its normal position; however, if the animal needs water, the skin is slow to return to normal. This same test can be used with people to determine the level of dehydration by pulling up on the skin for a few seconds and then releasing

it. If the skin doesn't immediately return to its original state, the person is dehydrated.

In Brain Gym, we use a similar method, but one that doesn't require you to pinch or pull your partner's skin. Instead, the person being checked pulls a small clump of his own hair and says "push" while he is being muscle checked. If his arm stays up, it means he has enough water and is hydrated. If it goes down, either he needs water or the person doing the muscle checking needs water. Therefore, if the arm does go down, the correction is for both of you to drink some water. Then repeat this muscle check by having your partner again pull his hair. Now his arm should easily stay up. Because some water molecules are absorbed in the mouth, it takes the body only a fifth of a second to register the fact that you have had a drink of water.

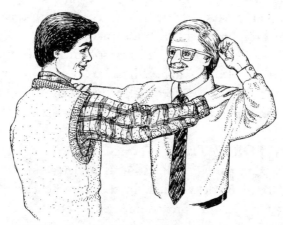

For Muscle Checking with a Partner: Ask your partner to pull a piece of his hair and, while he is pulling his hair, ask him to say "Pusssshhhhh" while you muscle check him. His arm should be switched-on.

If his arm is switched-off, both of you should drink some water and then repeat this muscle checking procedure. If the arm is still switched-off, both of you should take another sip of water and check again. Continue this procedure until the arm is switched-on.

## PART 3. ELECTRICAL CIRCUITRY:

Checking the electrical circuitry confirms that regardless of which hand you use to perform the muscle checking on your partner, you will get accurate answers. In essence what we're doing here is calibrating to make sure the person's body will give appropriate responses, no matter which hand is used to do the checking. If the person's arm goes down when you check electrical circuitry, the Brain Gym movement called Brain Buttons (page 61) is done as a correction.

For Muscle Checking with a Partner do steps below:

1. Place one hand on your partner's extended arm above the wrist bone and ask your partner to say "Pussss hhhh" as you do the muscle check.

2. Place your other hand on your partner's arm above the wrist bone and ask your partner to say "Pusssshhhhh" as you do the muscle check.

3. Once again, place your first hand on your partner's arm and ask your partner to say "Pusssshhhhh" as you do the muscle check. On Steps 3, 4, and 5 your partner's arm should remain switched-on.

If your partner's arm is switched-off on any of these three steps, stop here and both do Brain Buttons (see page 61). Then repeat Part 3 again. Your partner should now be switched-on for all three checks.

## PART 4. ACTIVATING:

In this part of Calibration, you are switching your system into gear to do the physical movements Brain Gym requires. You are activating your body to move. If the person's arm is switched-off on this step, the correction is doing 30 seconds of The Cross Crawl (page 65) and then re-checking to be sure the person is now switched-on for activity.

For Muscle Checking with a Partner do the steps below:

1. Ask your partner to use one of his fingers to find the bottom rib of his right rib cage at the place

where it comes to a point. This point is located a most in line with the arm pit.

2. Then ask him to move his finger straight up from that spot about two inches. This is where the Activating point is located and where you will be checking him.

3. Now have him release this point and place one of your fingers at this point. Ask your partner to say "Pussssh" as you do the muscle check on your partner. His arm should be switched-on.

If your partner's arm is switched-off on this step, stop here and both of you should do The Cross Crawl on page 65 for thirty seconds. Then repeat Part 4 again. Your partner should now be switched-on for this check.

## PART 5. STRESS REDUCTION:

In the Stress Reduction steps we muscle check the Central Meridian Line, which runs from the belly button area to the area below the lower lip. This is a different meridian line from the one I've shared with you so far. If the person gives an inappropriate response to this muscle check—for example, the arm stayed up when it should have come down—it means that she is over-energized. In the Switched-On Selling course I have added an additional method of Correction for Individuals Showing an Over-Energy Response that I believe is faster than Hook-ups and works most of the time. The instructions are below.

For Muscle Checking with a Partner do steps below:

1. "Zip Up" by tracing a line with your hand from your partner's belly button to his nose. Ask your partner to say "Pussssshhhhh"

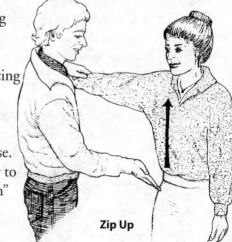

**Zip Up**

and do the muscle check. Your partner's arm should remain switched-on.

2. "Zip Down" by tracing a line with your hand from your partner's nose to his belly button. Ask your partner to say "Pusssshhhhh" and do the muscle check. Your partner's arm should be switched-off.

3. "Zip Up" again by tracing a line with your hand from your your partner's belly button to his nose without touching his body. Ask your partner to say "Pusssshhhhh" and do the muscle check. Your partner's arm should remain switched-on once again.

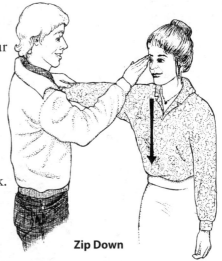

**Zip Down**

If your partner's arm gave an inconsistent response on the muscle checking for the "Zip Up" (it came down when it was supposed to stay up) or "Zip Down" (it stayed up when it was supposed to come down), then you should stop here and both of you do the Correction for Individuals Showing an Over-Energy Response, which is below. Then repeat Part 5 again. Your partner's muscle checking responses will most likely be appropriate now. If they are not appropriate, both of you should do the Brain Gym movement Hook-ups on page 63. Then repeat the muscle checking and it should be appropriate.

# CORRECTION FOR INDIVIDUALS SHOWING AN OVER-ENERGY RESPONSE

The Correction for Individuals Showing an Over-Energy Response is to do Hook-ups (see page 63). In addition, in Switched-On Selling there is another method of correction for this that works most of the time. This method was developed by Roger Callahan, Ph.D. and is taught in his book *Tapping the Healer Within*. Here are the instructions:

> *Ask the person to tap the fleshy part of the side of one hand, located just below the pinkie finger, against the same area on the other hand. This is the part of the hand that you would use to give a karate chop. She should do this 35 to 45 times.*

This simple activity seems to turn off the person's overactive adrenal glands for at least a short period of time, allowing you to get accurate muscle checking results. This tapping method works most of the time; however, if the muscle checking responses still do not match what the pattern should be in Part 5, have the person then do Hook-ups. After doing either Hook-ups or Tapping, the Stress Reduction process in Part 5 of Calibration should be appropriate in that the arm should stay up on each of the sweep-ups and go down on the sweep-down.

**PART 6. "YES"/"NO" RESPONSE:**

Have a partner muscle check you for "yes" or "no" responses on both of the following questions:

- "Your body will demonstrate a 'Yes' response." (Your arm should stay up.)
- "Your body will demonstrate a 'No' response." (Your arm should go down.)

By having completed Calibration you should get appropriate responses to both of these questions—switched-on for the "yes" and switched-off for the "no."

# APPENDIX B

## A Revolution in Training: The Bottom Line Results of The Switched-On Selling Seminar

### A Research Study With 695 Salespeople

BY

## DR. JERRY V. TEPLITZ

Jerry Teplitz Enterprises, Inc
1304 Woodhurst Drive
Virginia Beach, VA 23454
800 – 77-RELAX or 757 496-8008
FAX 757 496-9955
Email - Jerry@Teplitz.com
www.Teplitz.com

# CONTENTS

## Executive Summary

The Switched-On Selling (SOS) seminar was designed to allow participants to overcome their fears so that they can become successful salespeople. The SOS seminar is revolutionary because it does not teach any sales techniques. Rather, it teaches participants how to determine which areas of the selling process are causing him or her stress and difficulty. Then participants learn how to use movement exercises called Brain Gyms® to re-wire their brains so that they are able to adapt to new opportunities and changes.

This report presents the updating of an analysis conducted in 2001, when data from 365 participants' pre- and post-seminar questionnaires was compared to 61 participants who completed and returned the One-Month questionnaire. An analysis was conducted on all eighteen questions as well as on the Overall Response Total for all eighteen questions.

The updated group added data from 330 salespeople to the data in the original study, which provided data for a total of 695 participants. This group was compared to a group of 124 respondents who completed the questionnaire one month after the seminar.

Switched-On Selling seminar participants completed a self-assessment questionnaire before the seminar began, immediately after the seminar, and one month after attending the seminar. The responses to the initial questionnaire indicated how the participants viewed themselves in relationship to the selling process. Participants' responses to the questionnaire immediately after the seminar indicated whether the materials presented in the seminar changed their perceptions of themselves. Administering the questionnaire one month after the seminar determined whether the changes indicated on the second questionnaire were genuine and if they held.

The analysis shows that participants' self-perception of their sales ability improved dramatically at the end of the seminar. The analysis also shows that participant's positive perceptions about their sales abilities improved even further when they were back in the field selling.

This report also presents the results of an insurance company study that shows how the SOS seminar affects salespeople's bottom line. One team of salespeople in the company attended the seminar and another group did not. Salespeople who attended the SOS seminar increased sales 39 percent over those who did not attend the seminar. In addition, the group that attended the seminar increased their premium levels 71 percent over those who did not attend the seminar.

Finally, a pest control company put half of their sales force through the SOS seminar in June 2009, which was during the middle of the recession. Attendees were tracked for three months. One sales person had a 200 percent increase in sales. Company profits went up 25 percent and of the eight sales people who attended the seminar, six were now in the company's top tier of most successful salespeople.

## Introduction

What separates a top salesperson from an average salesperson? Why do some individuals seem to be born to sell while meeting a prospect is anathema to others? Scores of books, seminars, DVDs, and CDs are available to teach countless sales techniques. Yet, only a select few salespeople achieve the highest levels of sales success.

Could fear explain the gulf between success and failure in sales? Fear has a powerful effect on a person's behavior. When a person is functioning out of fear, he will attempt to avoid the cause of the fear. For example, if someone fears meeting people, he will not make calls or set up appointments. This occurs even though prospects would be interested in his product. As a result, the salesperson will not be successful and either will be a mediocre performer or eventually will resign.

The Switched-On Selling (SOS) seminar was designed to allow participants to overcome their fears so that they can become successful salespeople. The process developed for SOS uses a methodology that creates new neuron firing patterns in the brain in minutes. These new patterns allow salespeople to follow their company's training and move to new levels of sales success quickly and easily.

The SOS seminar is revolutionary because it does not teach any sales techniques. Instead, the seminar begins by using kinesiology, "an integrated system for assessing and evaluating the effects of all stimuli, internal and external, on the body, enabling us to arrive at a new understanding and synthesis of the integrative action of the body energy system."[1] Kinesiology muscle checking allows the seminar participant to determine which areas of the selling process are causing her stress and difficulty.

Once these areas of stress are identified, attendees are taught simple movement exercises called Brain Gyms®, which were originally developed Paul Dennison, Ph.D. and Gail Dennison to help children and adults with learning disabilities. The movement exercises are also designed to re-wire the brain from a fear/survival focus, which occurs

---

1  Definition from International Center for Nutritional Research, Inc.
   http://www.icnr.com/articles/behavioralkinesiology.html

in the back part of the brain and may be triggered by past experience, to a present-time/choice focus, which occurs in the front section of the brain. These Brain Gym® movements allow the brain to be open and be able to adapt to new opportunities and changes.

Dr. Jerry V. Teplitz, J.D., Ph.D. has adapted and applied these concepts to the sales process. The results of over nineteen years of research studies validating Brain Gym® can be read at www.Teplitz.com/BrainGymResearch.htm.

## The Switched-On Selling Study Methodology

Switched-On Selling Seminar participants completed a self-assessment questionnaire (See Appendix A) before the seminar began, immediately after the seminar, and one month after attending the seminar. The questionnaire that participants completed at the beginning of the day provided a baseline measurement of how the participants viewed themselves in relationship to the selling process. Completing the questionnaire again immediately after the seminar indicated whether the materials presented in the seminar changed their perceptions of themselves.

Participants were then asked to complete the questionnaire a final time one month later. This was designed to determine that the changes indicated on the second questionnaire were genuine and not the result of a seminar high, which occurs when a participant leaves a seminar motivated to change but returns to old behavioral patterns within days of the seminar's conclusion.

For the original analysis conducted in 2001, data from 365 participants' pre- and post-seminar questionnaires[2] was collected to provide the baseline measurement. This group was compared to 61 participants who completed and returned the One-Month questionnaire. An analysis was conducted on all eighteen questions as well as on the Overall Response Total for all eighteen questions (See end of Appendix for the questions).

---

2    These participants did not complete the One-Month questionnaire.

This revised study added data from 330 salespeople to the data in the original study, which provided data for a total of 695 participants. This group was compared to a group of 124 respondents who completed the questionnaire one month after the seminar. The analysis was also performed on all eighteen questions and on the Overall Response Total.

# ANALYSIS

## Original Study - Overall Response Totals

Figure 1 provides the results of the original study's pre- and post-seminar responses. On the pre-seminar questionnaire, 40 percent of the participants rated themselves negatively on their ability to be effective salespeople. At the end of the seminar, however, post-seminar results indicated that 92 percent of the participants believed that they were capable of performing all parts of the sales process. There were only 7 percent of the participants left on the negative side.

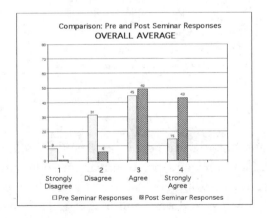

FIGURE I. ORIGINAL STUDY - OVERALL AVERAGE OF PRE- AND POST-SEMINAR RESPONSES

## Original Study - One Month Following the Seminar

The responses of participants who completed and returned the questionnaire one month after the seminar are presented in Figure 2. It illustrates that the participants not only continued to feel positive about their sales abilities at the end of the one-month follow-up period, but they improved even further. At the beginning of the seminar, 40 percent of the participants rated themselves negatively on their ability to be effective salespeople. After the seminar, 92 percent believed that they were capable of positively performing all parts of the sales process. One month later, 95 percent had a positive self-perception about their abilities as salespeople.

In addition, the number responding "Strongly Agree" increased from only 16 percent in that category at the beginning of the day to 43 percent at the end of the seminar and most dramatically to 55 percent on the one-month-later form. This means that when people were back in the field, they improved even further.

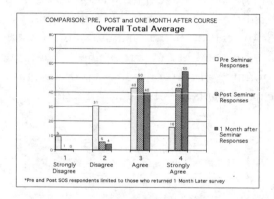

FIGURE 2. ORIGINAL STUDY - OVERALL AVERAGE OF RESPONSES ONE MONTH FOLLOWING SEMINAR

A high degree of correlation exists between the results of those who only completed the pre- and post-seminar questionnaires and those who completed the questionnaire all three times—before the seminar, immediately following, and one month after the seminar. Therefore, one can project that the responses of the One Month Later group are applicable to all the participants in the study.

Figure 3 provides the results of the revised study's pre- and post-seminar responses.[3] On the pre-seminar questionnaire, 38 percent

---

3   In the revised study, fractions were rounded, which sometimes resulted in a total of more or less than 100%.

of the participants rated themselves negatively on their ability to be effective salespeople. Post-seminar results indicate that 93 percent of the participants believed that they were capable of performing all parts of the sales process.

As mentioned earlier, the participants' changed self-perception at the conclusion of the seminar did not result from their learning new selling techniques at the seminar, but from using the Brain Gym movement exercises to create new response patterns.

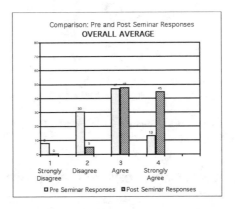

FIGURE 3. REVISED STUDY - OVERALL AVERAGE OF PRE- AND POST-SEMINAR RESPONSES

## Revised Study - One Month Following the Seminar

Figure 4 presents the responses of participants who completed the questionnaire one month after the seminar. As mentioned earlier, 38 percent of the participants rated themselves negatively on their ability to be effective salespeople when the seminar began. After the seminar, 93 percent believed that they were capable of performing all parts of the sales process. One month later, 93 percent had a positive self-perception about their abilities as salespeople. As in the original study, the revised study's results show that the participants continued to feel positive about their sales abilities when they were back in the field selling.

As in the original study, the participants' responses to "Strongly Agree" increased dramatically from 15 percent at the beginning of the day, to 43 percent at the end of the day, to 55 percent one month later.

This means that the results of the original study and the revised study are extremely consistent with each other. Due to this consistency, I will only refer to the results from the revised study's responses in analyzing the rest of the results.

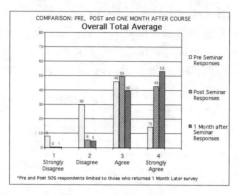

FIGURE 4. REVISED STUDY - OVERALL AVERAGE OF RESPONSES ONE MONTH FOLLOWING SEMINAR

## Responses to Select Questions Reveal Significant Changes

The responses to the following questions revealed the most significant changes in the participants' attitudes. We will now examine the first question:

*Question:* **I handle rejection well.**

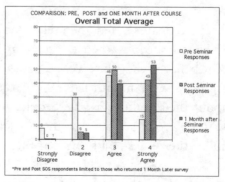

FIGURE 5. PRE- AND POST-SEMINAR RESPONSES: I HANDLE REJECTION WELL

Figure 5 illustrates responses to this statement on the pre- and post-seminar questionnaire. Sixty-four percent of participants responded negatively to this statement before the seminar. At the end of the seminar, only 9 percent of participants responded negatively. The post-seminar questionnaire responses also indicate that 90 percent of participants felt positive about their ability to handle rejection.

Figure 6 illustrates the responses of those who completed the questionnaire one month following the seminar. It shows that 89 percent of participants responded "Agree" or "Strongly Agree." The "Strongly Agree" category shows a 29 percent increase between the pre-seminar responses and the post-seminar responses and another 9 percent increase for follow-up one month later. Conversely, the "Disagree" or "Strongly Disagree" categories drop from 57 percent before the seminar to 9 percent one month after the seminar.

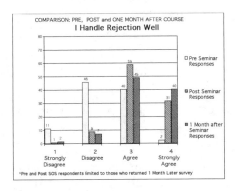

FIGURE 6. ONE MONTH FOLLOWING SEMINAR: I HANDLE REJECTION WELL

## *Question:* **It is easy for me to make cold calls in person.**

In Figure 7, 69 percent of the participants responded "Disagree" or "Strongly Disagree" to this statement on the pre-seminar questionnaire. One month later, only 13 percent responded the same. Only 29 percent responded "Agree" or "Strongly Agree" on the pre-seminar questionnaire. On the post-seminar questionnaire, however, 82 percent responded in kind. When participants returned to the field, the results of the follow-up questionnaire one month later show that their positive self-perception had continued to increase; 85 percent responded "Agree" or "Strongly Agree" to the statement. The "Strongly Agree" category also increased from 26 percent on the post-seminar questionnaire to 43 percent on the one-month-later questionnaire.

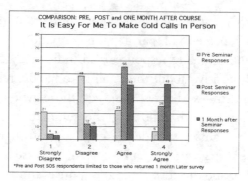

FIGURE 7. ONE MONTH FOLLOWING SEMINAR: IT IS EASY FOR ME TO MAKE COLD CALLS
    IN PERSON

## *Question:* It is easy for me to ask my clients for referrals.

Figure 8 illustrates responses to this statement. On the pre-seminar questionnaire, 47 percent of the participants responded "Disagree" or "Strongly Disagree" to this statement. On the post-seminar questionnaire, 6 percent of participants responded this way. One month later 6 percent still responded this way.

Fifty-one percent of participants responded "Agree" or "Strongly Agree" on the pre-seminar questionnaire. On the post-seminar questionnaire, however, 92 percent responded in kind. When participants returned to the field, the results of the follow-up questionnaire show that they continued to have a positive self-perception one month later; 92 percent continued to respond "Agree" or "Strongly Agree." The "Strongly Agree" category grew from only 10 percent on the pre questionnaire to 36 percent on the post one and to 48 percent on the one-month-later responses.

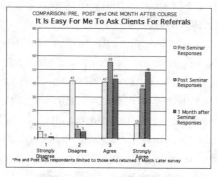

FIGURE 8. ONE MONTH FOLLOWING SEMINAR: IT IS EASY FOR ME TO ASK CLIENTS
    FOR REFERRALS

## Statistical Analysis

A statistical analysis was performed on the results from the pre- and post-seminar questionnaires and the questionnaires completed one month after the seminar. The analysis of variance of the three levels yielded an F-ratio of 122.76 (df=2, 120), which is significant beyond the .0001 level. It indicates that there is a significant difference among the three test periods.

A subsequent test, the Newman-Keuls Analysis, revealed that the post-seminar and one-month follow-up questionnaires did not differ from each other but that both of them differed from the pre-seminar questionnaire. In other words, the Switched-On Selling seminar had a significant effect on the participants between the first and second time they completed the form, down to the .0001 level. A statistically significant difference between the post-seminar and one-month follow-up was not found. The hypothesis points to the fact that the seminar had a significant and sustaining effect on participants.

## Two Field Studies Show How SOS Seminar Affects Bottom Line

Although the graphs in this report indicate that salespeople's self-perceptions change significantly as a result of attending the Switched-On Selling seminar, salespeople are most interested in learning how these changes correlate to bottom-line dollars.

To discover how the SOS seminar affects salespeople's bottom line, the South Carolina Farm Bureau, an insurance company, conducted its own study. Its sales force was divided into two groups, one that attended the seminar, and one that did not.

The company tracked both groups for four months after the seminar and compared everyone's sales figures from the previous year against those from the current year. Salespeople who attended the SOS seminar increased sales 39 percent over those who did not attend the seminar.

For insurance agents, the figure for increased premiums is considered even more important than overall sales. The results demonstrated that the group that attended the seminar increased their premium levels 71 percent over those who did not attend the seminar.

The second company was A-Active Termite and Pest Control Company, a pest control company located in Virginia Beach, Virginia. The President, Kevin Kordek, attended a seminar I conducted on *Increasing Your Leadership Power To New Levels Of Excellence* for his Entrepreneur Organization Hampton Roads Chapter. Kordek decided to have me conduct my both my Switched-On Selling and Switched-On Management training seminars for his staff.

With the Switched-On Selling (SOS) seminar, he decided to initially put half of his sales force through the seminar in June 2009. As you may recall, this was during the middle of the recession. Attendees were tracked for three months after the seminar. As Kordek says, the results were spectacular! One sales person had a 200 percent increase in sales, while company profits went up 25 percent. Of the eight sales people who attended the seminar, six were now in the company's top tier of most successful salespeople.

The interesting thing is several of the staff who went through the SOS Seminar initially thought that the seminar had done nothing. It took looking at their statistics after three months for them to realize that the only thing that would account for the dramatic level of change they were experiencing was having attended the seminar.

All these positive changes occurred while the rest of the pest industries business had been contracting. Kordek has now put his remaining sales force through the seminar and initial results look to be similar to the first group's experience.

To arrange for your sales force to attend a Switched-On Selling Seminar, call 800-77-RELAX or visit www.Teplitz.com and click on Switched-On Seminars, the click on Find an Instructor section.

To read the rest of the Switched-On Selling Research report, you can go online to www.Teplitz.com/BrainGymResearch.htm. In addition, at this Web site you will find a Research Report on the impact of Switched-On Selling conducted for bankers. There is also a sister seminar for Network Marketers that has this research published at the site.

Lastly, there is an seminar that uses the Brain Gym process to impact managers. It is called Switched-On Management, and a pilot study on its impact can be found on the same site.

# SOS Pre- and Post-Course Questionnaire

| | | Strongly Agree | Agree | Disagree | Strongly Disagree |
|---|---|---|---|---|---|
| 1. | I handle rejection well. | | | | |
| 2. | I research potential clients prior to contacting. | | | | |
| 3. | I enjoy selling. | | | | |
| 4. | I am effective as a salesperson. | | | | |
| 5. | I view myself as a successful salesperson. | | | | |
| 6. | It is easy for me to make cold calls using the telephone. | | | | |
| 7. | It is easy for me to make cold calls in person. | | | | |
| 8. | I am comfortable talking on the telephone. | | | | |
| 9. | I am comfortable with face-to-face visits. | | | | |
| 10. | I develop a rapport quickly with a client. | | | | |
| 11. | I effectively begin the presentation. | | | | |
| 12. | I effectively answer objections and questions. | | | | |
| 13. | I am comfortable asking for the order and closing the sale. | | | | |
| 14. | It is easy for me to write proposals. | | | | |
| 15. | I provide effective customer service. | | | | |
| 16. | It is easy for me to ask my clients for referrals. | | | | |
| 17. | I offer clients other opportunities. | | | | |
| 18. | I view myself as prosperous. | | | | |

# APPENDIX C

## Executive Summaries from Other Research

The follow are Executive Summaries of other research studies conducted by Dr. Teplitz on the impact of other Switched-On training seminars:

### Switched-On Selling Seminar Research for Bankers Report

People going into banking don't usually view themselves as salespeople. When they are put into positions where they have to sell, many quickly discover the challenges of selling. While they can read books, attend seminars, watch DVDs, and listen to CDs to learn sales techniques, only a few achieve the highest levels of sales success. Until now...

Our study indicates that powerful changes occurred for 87 participants from five banks who had attended the one-day Switched-On Selling seminar (SOS). Each seminar was conducted at different times and locations. Another more in-depth study of 695 salespeople from all types of sales positions achieved very similar results.

Using self-evaluation forms that were completed by the participants at the beginning and at the end of the seminar, our study showed that a banker's self-perception of his or her sales ability improved very dramatically by the end of the SOS seminar. A number of the participants also completed a third self-evaluation form one month later. Reviewing that data showed even further improvement once the participants were back on the job at their banks.

**To read the entire report, go to**
**www.Teplitz.com/BrainGymResearch.html**

## Switched-On Network Marketing Seminar Research Report

The Switched-On Network Marketing (SONM) seminar was designed to allow participants to overcome their fears so that they can become successful network marketers.

This report presents the results of a seventeen-item self-assessment questionnaire that 95 SONM participants answered before the seminar, immediately after the seminar, and one month after the seminar. The analysis showed that participants experienced very positive outcomes and dramatically altered their view of themselves in relationship to the network marketing process by the end of the seminar. The results one month later found that the changes not only held but that they actually improved even further.

**To read the entire report, go to**
**www.Teplitz.com/BrainGymResearch.html**

## Switched-On Network Management Seminar Research Report

The Switched-On Management (SOM) seminar is a practical self-development management training program for managers to create a more successful, effective, and dynamic company or organization. SOM is designed to help managers become more effective with management skills they have and develop skills in new areas of management.

This report presents the results of a pilot study conducted on the impact of the SOM seminar. For this study, 21 SOM participants completed a self-assessment questionnaire before the seminar began and again at the end of the seminar. The questionnaire that participants completed at the beginning of the seminar provided a baseline measurement of how the they viewed themselves in relationship to the various parts of the management process. The questionnaire that participants completed at the end of the seminar indicated whether the seminar had changed their perception of themselves.

The responses to pre- and post-seminar questionnaires indicate that seminar participants' self-perception of their management ability increased significantly at the conclusion of the seminar.

**To read the entire report, go to**
**www.Teplitz.com/BrainGymResearch.html**

## Brain Gym Annotated Research Chronology

The Brain Gym Foundation has posted on its Web site a research report summarizing twenty-plus years of Brain Gym research.

**To read the complete report, go to**
**www.BrainGym.org**

# BIOGRAPHIES

## Dr. Tony Alessandra

Dr. Tony Alessandra has a street-wise, college-smart perspective on business, having been raised in the housing projects of NYC to eventually realizing success as a graduate professor of marketing, entrepreneur, business author, and hall-of-fame keynote speaker. He earned a BBA from the University of Notre Dame, an MBA from the University of Connecticut and his PhD in marketing from Georgia State University.

In addition to being president of Assessment Business Center, a company that offers online 360° assessments, Tony is also a founding partner in The Cyrano Group and Platinum Rule Group—companies which have successfully combined cutting-edge technology and proven psychology to give salespeople the ability to build and maintain positive relationships with hundreds of clients and prospects.

Dr. Alessandra is a prolific author with 19 books translated into over 50 foreign language editions, including the newly revised, best selling *The NEW Art of Managing People* (Free Press/Simon & Schuster, 2008); *Charisma* (Warner Books, 1998); *The Platinum Rule* (Warner Books, 1996); *Collaborative Selling* (John Wiley & Sons, 1993); and *Communicating at Work* (Fireside/Simon & Schuster, 1993). He is featured in over 100 audio/video programs and films, including *Relationship Strategies* (American Media); *The Dynamics of Effective Listening* (Nightingale-Conant); and *Non-Manipulative Selling* (Walt Disney). He is also the originator of the internationally recognized behavioral style assessment tool, The Platinum Rule®.

Recognized by *Meetings & Conventions Magazine* as "one of America's most electrifying speakers," Dr. Alessandra was inducted into the Speakers Hall of Fame in 1985 and is a member of the Speakers Roundtable, a group of 20 of the world's top professional speakers. Tony's polished style, powerful message, and proven ability as a consummate business strategist consistently earn rave reviews and loyal clients.

Contact information for Dr. Tony Alessandra:
- Dr. Tony's products:
  http://www.alessandra.com/products/index.asp
- Online Assessments: Brandon Parker: Phone: 1-760-872-1500
  Email: BParker@ParkerWebSolutions.com
- Keynote Speeches: Holli Catchpole: Phone: 1-760-603-8110
  Email: Holli@SpeakersOffice.com
- Corporate Training: Scott Zimmerman:
  Phone: 1-330-848-0444, x2
  Email: Scott@PlatinumRule.com
- Cyrano CRM System: Scott Zimmerman:
  Phone: 1-330-848-0444, x2
  Email: Scott@PlatinumRule.com

# DR. JERRY V. TEPLITZ

Dr. Jerry V. Teplitz' background is as unique as the techniques and approaches he teaches. He is a graduate of Hunter College and Northwestern University School of Law and practiced as an attorney for the Illinois Environmental Protection Agency.

Jerry's career took a dramatic change of direction when he received Masters and Doctorate Degrees in Wholistic Health Sciences from Columbia Pacific University. He was on the faculty of the U.S. Chamber of Commerce Institute for Organization Management for nine years.

Recently in the association industry, Dr. Teplitz' expertise has been recognized by speaking engagements at such prestigious organizations as the Professional Convention Management Association Annual Convention, the American Society of Association Executives (ASAE) Great Ideas Conference, the ASAE's Annual Convention, and the Canadian Society of Association Executives Annual Convention.

Dr. Teplitz had been a field manager for the Inscape Publishing Company for thirty years and president of his own consulting firm for over thirty-five years. Jerry conducts seminars in the areas of stress management, employee productivity, and sales development.

The list of clients Dr. Teplitz has spoken to and consulted for includes such organizations as IBM, Motorola, FDIC, and Time, Inc. In addition, he has spoken to Century 21, Holiday Inns, International Management Council, Young Presidents' Organization, Associated General Contractors, GlaxoSmithKline, American Bankers Association, plus over four hundred colleges and universities across the United States and Canada.

Dr. Teplitz has been a Brain Gym 101 Instructor since 1986. He served on the Brain Gym International Board of Directors for nine years and chaired the Brain Gym Marketing Committee. Jerry is the creator of the *Switched-On Selling, Management,* and *Network Marketing* Seminars and Instructor Certification training programs. He also assisted in the original development of the *Switched-On Golf* Seminar and is certified to teach it.

Jerry is the author of *Managing Your Stress In Difficult Times* and *Switched-On Living.* He co-authored *Brain Gym for Business* with the founders of Brain Gym, Dr. Paul Dennison and Gail Dennison. Articles on Jerry have appeared in such publications as *Successful Meetings, Prevention,* and *Travel and Leisure Golf* magazines. He has also been listed in several editions of Who's Who in America.

As a professional speaker, he has spoken to over one million people. Dr. Teplitz has also been honored by his peers in the National Speakers Association by earning the title of Certified Speaking Professional (CSP) and has been selected by Professional Convention Management Association as "Best-in-Class" speaker based on the quality and impact of his presentations.

Contact information for Dr. Jerry Teplitz:
- Dr. Jerry's products: www.Teplitz.com/Catalog.html
- Keynote speeches and seminars: 1-757-496-8008
  Email: Info@Teplitz.com
- Switched-On Selling seminar and instructor training:
  www.Teplitz.com/switched-main.htm
  Email: Info@Teplitz.com

# NORMA ECKROATE

Norma Eckroate has co-authored numerous books for humans and animals. With Dr. Jerry V. Teplitz, she also coauthored *Switched-On Living: Easy Ways to Use the Mind/Body Connection to Energize Your Life.*

An advocate for the compassionate nonviolent treatment of animals, her books include three titles with Paul Owens, who is referred to as the "original" Dog Whisperer: *The Dog Whisperer, The Puppy Whisperer,* and the newly released *The Dog Whisperer Presents Good Habits for Great Dogs.*

Norma has also written extensively on holistic health, including coauthoring Anitra Frazier's bestselling *The Natural Cat,* which has been called the "Bible" of natural cat care (also published under the title *The New Natural Cat*). With Dr. Mary Brennan, Norma coauthored *The Natural Dog* and *Complete Holistic Care and Healing for Horses.*

Norma's work recently took a turn to the more magical aspects of life with the publication of *The Santa Story Revisited: How to Give Your Children a Santa They Will Never Outgrow,* coauthored with Arita Trahan (Downstream Enterprises, 2009).

In addition to writing, Norma has worked extensively in both theatre and television. Most recently, she produced Paul Owens' Dog Whisperer DVDs, *The Dog Whisperer: Beginning and Intermediate Dog Training* and *The Dog Whisperer, Vol. 2: Solving Common Behavior Problems for Puppies and Dogs.*

Norma has a B.A. in dramatic arts from Kent State University and an M.A. in metaphysical science from the University of Sedona. She is a licensed spiritual practitioner at the Agape International Spiritual Center in Culver City, California, and also teaches metaphysics and spirituality.

Contact information for Norma Eckroate:
- *Dog Whisperer* books, DVDs and free advice: www.DogWhispererDVD.com
- *The Natural Cat:* www.TheNaturalCat.net
- *The Santa Story Revisited:* www.TheSantaStory.com

# INDEX

# Testimonials from Switched-On Selling Seminar Participants

"I always knew what I should be doing to get the sale. I even knew how to get the sale. But my fear made it impossible to keep a good relationship with my clients. When we first began the seminar I was very skeptical and unsure it would work for me. However, right away I could notice differences in my attitudes and realized that my thoughts that were more positive. All the negative seemed to be crowded out. After about a week, I felt fearless and unstoppable with a new sense of direction. Last, but certainly not least, my sales have increased four-fold!"

—Patricia Cole, Riddle, OR

"I thoroughly enjoyed the seminar and I know I gained knowledge and insight I will use on a daily basis. I thought the changes manifested in most of the participants by the end of the seminar were nothing short of remarkable."

—Kay W. Hurley, Tidewater Builders Association, Chesapeake, VA

"Your seminar is one of the most useful seminars I have ever attended in terms of giving me immediate help. Since taking the seminar I have been able to use the Brain Gym exercises to make sales calls much less stressful. I have used the exercises to remove the dread of coming to work on the days I know won't be pleasant."

—J. Marty Godfrey, Executive Vice President
Appalachian Community Bank, Blairsville, GA

"Prior to Switched-On Selling, setting goals was difficult. Since the workshop I easily set my goals and I review and visualize them daily!"

—Julia Lewis, San Jose, CA

"Wow! After the Switched-On Selling seminar I made a decision to increase my business income. And the last year has seen a 50% increase to the bottom line. I am thrilled! Anytime a business of 15 years can grow by 50% in just one year is remarkable."

—Sherry Knight, President, Dimension 11, Ltd.,
Regina, Saskatchewan, Canada

"When I took the Switched-On Selling class, I worked at a radio station where I needed a certain amount in sales to get bonuses. After the class, I far surpassed what I needed. After I was transferred to another station, the sales at my previous station dropped $4,000 a month. This class helps right away and its benefits are long term."

—Rose Romero, Colorado Springs, CO

"Your techniques have had a strong impact on my life. At first I was extremely skeptical. However, since taking your Switched-On Selling seminar I am a firm believer in what it can do for myself and others. I have been in sales for the last 10 years of my life. Yet there had always been a lingering fear in me to proceed. Since taking your course, I have the confidence and ability to move forward. In addition, there was a time or two that I felt quite upset and stressed. After doing the Brain Gym exercises I was feeling so much calmer. Thank you so much for helping to make such a huge impact in my life."

—Joel Saxe, Independent Global Marketing Executive,
New Economy International, LLC, Portland, OR

"I now talk more easily and confidently with strangers and find myself making cold calls with ease. In fact, I'm not shy to suggest additional publications when people contact me to order a specific book, and have often marveled at my newfound ease with 'selling'!"

—Denise Cambiotti, Coquitlam, British Columbia, Canada

"My reason for taking your seminar was to try to overcome my call reluctance, which I had struggled with for over eighteen years. My state of mind at the close of the seminar was dramatically altered from when it began. After the seminar it became necessary to 'get on the phone' and book appointments for presentations. The ease with which I was able to make those calls and the positive responses that I received from the people I called was truly amazing. Literally a 100% positive response to the calls made, all appointments booked, and all presentations completed.

"This seminar has completely changed my feeling of self-esteem and self-worth and is quite vividly evident in the response I am getting from the people I am contacting. The seminars you offer are literally 'life changing' and produce noticeable positive results basically immediately."

—Jay Horton, Calgary, Alberta, Canada

"My fear of failure was so great that I literally scared people away. The seek following the seminar, I did a Seven minute tune-up each day. After about 10 days I was making phone calls and talking to people as never before. My confidence and zeal were back much bigger and better than before. Even though some of my old fears come up even now, I am able to consistently override them without a great deal of effort. What a great relief! The most tangible result is that my sales have quadrupled in the last six months."

—Julie Metzler

"I'm amazed at how easy it is to approach people and start talking to them. It is easier to discuss and ask for money. Thanks."

—Ruth Upchurch, Woodstock, GA

"You helped me overcome a problem that's hindered me for most of my adult life. Your 'silly little exercises' helped me blow away that hang up which was my reluctance to write things down, specifically, goals. What's amazing to me is that I have no idea where this problem originated. I always thought the only way to get rid of irrational fears and phobias was to discover their origin and work from that knowledge. Your approach clearly refutes that. I can honestly say your work has helped enhance both my business and personal lives."

—Ahron Katz, President, A-abc Appliance and Air Conditioning, Dallas, TX

"Since I took your Switched-On Selling seminar, I want to tell you about one of the most amazing techniques I learned—positive points! It works every time I want to get rid of negative feeling or judgment. It's magic."

—Whitney Foster, Health Resource Center, Virginia Beach, VA

"Thanks for the Switched-On Selling course—it has really helped me. I followed through with the exercises and really felt when things switched over for good. Now if I start to slip a little, the exercises kick it back in quickly. This has been very effective for me and I continue to learn and work with the process. Thanks again!"

—Kim Auten, Ogden, UT

"The course was GREAT! After being in sales for years, I found blocks I had no idea I had. Now that I have removed those blocks, life and work are certainly more fun. I find myself doing the right things at the right time instinctively."

—Joan Langevin, Realty Executives, Virginia Beach, VA

"Thank you for your Switched-On Selling seminar. I never expected any single event to bring about such a profound change in my life. In fact, if someone had told me the impact it would have, I never would have believed it! Now I find myself far more focused; I know exactly what needs to be done because my goals are written down and clearly defined. All of that spells a marked improvement in my production."

—Lucia Occhiuzzo, Dallas, Texas

"Before I completed your course, I was averaging one insurance sale a week, and then afterward it went up to 3.5 sales a week. After five months of maintaining this level, I changed companies and my sales increased even more dramatically. After my first five weeks, I was the top agent in the office."

—Veda Stone, Insurance Salesperson, Virginia Beach, VA

"The day after the seminar, the results were instantaneous. We closed seven contracts, seven times more than we had done during the preceding eight months. By the end of the week, we had eighteen signed contracts."

—Serge Gravelle, Webmaster, Largo, FL

"The Switched-On Selling experience had the greatest impact in the shortest period of time of any program I have seen in my many years in sales management."

—Robert E. Donovan, Director of Life Sales,
The Independent Order of Foresters, San Diego, CA

"I just had to write and thank you for your Switched-On Selling seminar. I never experienced a single event to bring about such a profound change in my life. In fact, if someone had told me the impact it would have on me, I would never have believed it!"

—Lucia Occhiuzzo, Financial Advisor, Dallas, TX

"What was great about your program is you showed sales reps how to reprogram their thinking so they are highly effective. This should be a required seminar before anyone takes traditional sales training. You have found the missing piece!"

—Andy Miller, Sales Trainer, Sandler Training Institute, McLean, VA

"Since taking your seminar, I feel much more relaxed about selling and notice an inner confidence that's just 'there.' I'm setting my goals more consciously for selling each day and feel wonderful about it. I thank you, Jerry, for your excellent material!"

—Sabina DeVita, Brampton, Ontario Canada

"WOW! The Switched-On Selling seminar was outstanding and, judging from our evaluation forms, our staff all thought so as well. The best part about the training is that results are instantaneous. SOS is an entirely new approach to sales training and one our group enjoyed and embraced. Our staff left the training with a positive view of selling."

—Jack W. Shuler, President & CEO, Pee Dee Farm Credit, Florence, SC